F.C. Ta___
_____ olla, Mo.

Febr. 19, 1954

CHRISTIANITY, DIPLOMACY AND WAR

The Beckly Social Service Lecture

CHRISTIANITY, DIPLOMACY AND WAR

by

HERBERT BUTTERFIELD

M.A. (Cambridge), Hon. LL.D. (Aberdeen),
Fellow of Peterhouse and Professor of Modern History
in the University of Cambridge

ABINGDON-COKESBURY PRESS
NEW YORK   .   NASHVILLE

CONTENTS

ONE

CHRISTIANITY AND HUMAN PROBLEMS

THERE are a number of reasons why those who try to do their thinking as Christians may legitimately hope to make some contribution toward the solving of the world's problems. And though the attempt may be unsuccessful on any particular occasion, the same reasons always impose upon the Christian the duty of trying to break through the conventional framework of contemporary thinking on those subjects.

In the first place there have accumulated around the Christian tradition various forms of worldly wisdom which condense the experience of centuries and have come to stand as part of our European heritage. For nearly two thousand years our religion has particularly represented and upheld the element of continuity in our civilization. Even in matters that are of merely mundane concern, the historical Church has tended to cherish the long-term precepts, the truths that span the ages. It is true that the weight of so long a past—the drag of so much history which Christianity carries behind it—has had many disadvantages, especially at the very point where religion plays its part in public affairs. A tradition misunderstood, or inflexibly interpreted, is no doubt always one of the most sinister of the dangers which can menace an historical Church. Yet in the business of a nation, or a European order, or a civilized world, it is fatal to disregard one particular kind of tradition—namely, those maxims of conduct which embody the results of man's long-term experience on the earth. A certain sagacity in this part of our Christian heritage—though occasionally it has been regarded by churchmen almost as evidence for the rightness of the religion itself—has owed some of its virtue to the workings of time and the continuity of a single experience which ripens and corrects itself through a succession of centuries. The benefits of this accumulated wisdom can never be gathered by the mere reading of history books; for what a man gets out of history depends only too often upon what he first puts into it; and one can so re-write the story of mankind that all its tendency is to ratify those errors which happen to be current at the present day. On the other hand, it is true that many of the maxims which were once associated with the Christian outlook underwent a secularization at the time when the world began to shake itself free of religion. Those which concern international affairs came down to us therefore rather as traditions of European diplomacy, and we have ended by losing sight of some of the Christian assumptions which really lay behind them. Let us say, then, that the twentieth century has made some serious breaches— and amongst these possibly some desirable breaches— with the traditions of European diplomacy, for example. The Christian—still somewhat the guardian of the continuities in our civilization—may be concerned to inquire whether anything valuable is being thrown away at the same time.

At the opposite extreme we may ask in the second place whether, in spite of appearances, Christianity is not eminently capable of producing the greatest breach of tradition—precipitating the unpredictable thing. We may wonder whether the Christian does not find himself in the middle of a set of relationships calculated to catapult him to some interesting point in space where new perspectives will give him a glimpse of new things. If he is attached to long-term traditions the world is apt to lock itself into short-term ones, and is slow to break through the intellectual framework of a mere generation. Its thoughts often go on revolving only within that framework, and turning in on themselves, while men vainly imagine that they are producing something new. The world, moreover, trembles as though confronted with the spectre of bankruptcy if the intellectual framework even shows signs of breaking down as the result of its own defects. Precisely because he can hold fast to spiritual truths—not turning any mundane programme or temporal ideal into the absolute of absolutes—the Christian has it in his power to be more flexible in respect of all subordinate matters, and to ally himself with whatever may be the best for the world at a given moment. In the last resort he can clear away all intermediate systems and meet an unprecedented problem by going back to his starting-point—his zeal for personalities as such. It is open to him to unload himself of all the intervening years and even to cut through the traditions of historical Christianity, so that all may be fluid and flexible save that ultimate Rock, which is Christ Himself. He may, for example, return to the Sermon on the Mount or the Gospel narrative, and confront the twentieth century with the original simplicities of the faith. In the time of the greatest stress and the darkest tragedy this may be the only means by which human values themselves are likely to be re-established. Even amongst men who would hardly claim to be numbered with original thinkers, the policy of referring back to the primary Christian truths may precipitate new things and prove to be a starting-point of historical change. In the sixteenth century those who insisted that Christ had come to make men free helped to secure that modern sectarianism should be the parent of political liberty. In a similar context the ideals of communism and egalitarianism were introduced to the modern world.

Like our predecessors in so many generations, we are

often tempted to think that the order of things in which we live—or some such revision of it as we have already compassed in our imagination, so that we can almost reach it with our finger-tips—will always be the best thing possible for the world, preserving just those values to which we are attached at the present moment. Like our forefathers in the age of aristocracies, we cannot believe that an order of things which we have not imagined or promoted may bring new values, new patterns of human life, and new benefits to the human race, under a set of conditions that is beyond our foresight. Yet while men weep to see the end of the things they love, something in Christianity survives the fall of Roman Empires and national monarchies, lives on when Platonism and Aristotelianism go out of fashion, and persists when a whole civilization changes its character. The Christian is particularly called to carry his thinking outside that framework which a nation or a political party or a social system or an accepted régime or a mundane ideology provides. Even the preservation of what we may love as the existing order of things—even Anglo-Saxon ideals and western values—are not the absolute absolutes for the Christian. It is always possible, therefore, that a return to the first principles of our religion will once again precipitate upon the world a new thing.

It may be argued, however, that if traditionalism can run to excess, originality itself and the breach with tradition—the leap into the unpredictable—possess perils of their own. And no doubt Christianity in its essence is a risky religion, packed with the kind of ethical implications that are dangerous to status quo's, established régimes, and reigning systems. Perhaps we ought to impute a far more considerable role in history than we usually do—and ascribe a far more damaging influence— to those people who perform the function of making

Christianity a safe religion, accommodating it to the existing order of the world, and rendering it more compliant toward the powers that be. They are the agency through which the Church came to be hated as the instrument of tyranny; and they would seem to have operated as one of the primary causes of its decline. Even within the normal routine of historical Christianity, however, there is the basis for a third reason why the Christian should attempt to be independent in thought, and should let his Christianity do his thinking for him. Certain aspects of Christian teaching—the treatment of love, the insistence on humility, the attitude to human personality and the doctrine of sin—have helped to affect the character of our civilization, no doubt, but still leave a divergence between the message of the Church and the assumptions which are current in the world. Through direct reference to such a teaching, many Christians, for example, have played a distinguished part by their care for the suffering —even the suffering of their enemies—in time of war.

In general, I think that in time of war we should expect the Christian to have compassion somewhere even for the enemy, and even for the wicked—expect him also to be diffident about believing that his own nation's cause is absolutely the righteous one, and all the wickedness on the side of the enemy. And, important though it always is to win a war, we should expect the Christian to be diffident about believing that the fate of God and all His angels in all the future is going to depend on the Greeks beating the Trojans in one age of history, or on Russia rather than Germany dominating the continent in another age of history. The Christian has principles which can rescue him from the blindness of mere partisanship— principles which come like a compassionate wing to cover the whole of this wilful and distracted human race. Without being either traditionalist or revolutionary, but

merely by following a course that is currently recognized
—following a principle to which all men do lip-service—
he has a chance of performing a role of the highest
strategic importance at the present day.

In *The Listener* for 21st September 1950, Professor
James Welch examines the position of those Africans 'who
still need the best the British have to offer, and equally
resent needing it'. He particularizes the case which the
Africans make against the British, and enumerates the
complaints which we have to raise in return; and the
result is a startling example of argument at a deadlock,
argument at cross-purposes. He continues:

Only a few days ago I heard a West African putting before
a sympathetic group of British the feelings and convictions of
his people and the reasons for their hostility to Britain; and I
heard him answered by a typical and sincere Englishman who
is entirely devoted to the African and wholly given to serving
him. And as I heard that good Englishman, from the best of
motives, criticize Africans for what he believed was their own
good, I was filled with despair. For . . . all his desire to help the
African was of no avail in making him *feel with* the African
in what he had been saying. The gulf between the two
remained. Neither was able to move a step toward the other.
Communication had broken down.

And the author of this article asks the question which
is bound to preoccupy all Christians at the present
moment:

Is there a creative way out of this *impasse*? Can a bridge be
built between the two points of view sincerely held by sincere
people? . . . Is there a way of life, a philosophy, which is
essentially personalist, giving primacy of importance to human
persons, and, at the same time, free from racial and colour
conflict and prejudice? . . . No problem of human relations,
however intractable it may seem, is insoluble to genuine
Christian love.

When Mr Welch speaks of the *impasse* to which we come in our relations with the West Africans, we can add, within the lifetime of most of us, the parallel cases of the Irish, the Egyptians, the Indians, the Malayans, and others. In international relations the deadlocks are only too liable to be of precisely the same kind; and before any powers take the decision to resort to war there is a point where the argument has come to a similar *impasse*, and there is a gulf which human imagination has failed to bridge.

In view of his awareness of the streak of egotism in human beings, no Christian will dare to assert that all the world's quarrels are to be solved by human understanding. Human understanding is urgently needed as a preliminary, however, and it is essential to recognize the fact that there are problems of human relations which the intellect of man has never yet been able to grasp. Throughout history we see dark screens that stand as barriers to international comprehension—we see sincere men, only too conscious of their good intentions, but locked in their separate worlds and arguing woefully at cross-purposes. If all men were to become as unselfish as St Francis, and were to do so in time to remove the present causes of stumbling, the problems would be solved, and a profound Christian message would be vindicated. Short of that, however, it is our duty to see that life in the world shall be as tolerable as we can make it; and some of the problems that are involved in the relations between peoples are problems addressed to our thought and our imagination. Here is an area of human life not yet brought under intellectual control, but amenable to it sooner or later if we try to exceed our present state. It seems to be the case that even the historian, remote from our passions and preoccupations, may need a long period before he masters the particular intellectual hurdles which our generation failed to surmount. I personally have no doubt that he will ultimately get over them, and perhaps even—though often too glibly—point out what wiser courses we might have pursued. I imagine that the thing the general historian would say about the barriers to international understanding would be that they go much more deep than is generally assumed, so that at any given moment we underestimate the effort that is needed to secure their dislodgement. We underestimate how far we have come short of what is necessary for a genuine understanding of the other party's case. There is urgent need for us to convince ourselves, however, that mere historical knowledge does not ever suffice to surmount the obstacle. As many of us know, a long period of service, however self-sacrificing, in India or in Africa may still leave a man in an attitude of 'Blimpishness'. It is not sufficient to have researchers in Germany or gatherers of information in Russia. We may listen as the African himself makes his explanations, and we still may not understand, because we are unable to feel with him—we do not give something of ourselves in order to achieve real apprehension. And in fact we all know that the barriers can exist between parties within the same nation, and even a man and wife may be blocked in the effort of understanding. There is a sense in which it would be proper, therefore, to describe most of our thinking in these fields as still somewhat at the pre-Copernican stage; for we have not sufficiently examined, or sufficiently allowed for, that totally unconscious bias in the vision of both the Englishman and the foreigner—the bias which arises from what I can only call the position and the state of the observer.

The problem is one, therefore, which calls not merely for knowledge but also for imagination. And like the proper study of history it requires a certain giving of ourselves—requires in fact that we shall do something with our personalities. What society needs is every possible variation and extension of the art of putting oneself—and actually feeling oneself—in the other person's place. And this process, which is the most difficult in the world, has an unfortunate way of appearing to be the easiest, especially to the honest man who is a partisan. Those who are farthest from possessing the capacity to achieve it are—by that self-same defect—the ones most incapable of realizing the fact. Yet a person who is inadequate in this—however brilliant he may be in other ways—is totally incompetent for the solution of our particular problem. While we perfect our atomic bombs we are not always aware that we are required with equal urgency to increase our very stature—for it cannot be too often stated that it is human understanding itself which needs to be enlarged. And since it means thinking with our sympathies, and actually feeling with the other party —means giving something of our personalities so that we may comprehend the men not like-minded with ourselves —it is to Christian thought in particular that the problem is most likely to be presented. Little by little we may hope that Christian thought will turn into communicable knowledge those forms of intellectual exploration which are accessible only to men in a certain frame of mind, to human beings in love, human beings willing to make fools of themselves for love.

A comparatively small number of communists, possessing initially no measurable degree of power, achieved in the thirty years after 1917 such a transformation of the globe as has rarely been equalled in magnitude or in thoroughness or in extent. They achieved far more than all the armies of Kaiser and Tsar, of British and Austro-Hungarian

Empires, and of the United States, put together. Above all, what they achieved was to a far greater degree what they had intended than had been the case with any of the alliances or the governments which were in operation at that time. Indeed, with the partial exception of that other rebel, De Valera, no other statesman or party then functioning ever came so near to producing the kind of world offered in a political programme or promised to the public—came so near to keeping control over the consequences of policy.

All those people who are driven to pessimism and paralysis by the idea that nothing can be effected on this earth save by numbers and power, may take comfort, therefore, from this exhilarating example. The reading of abridged text-books has the grave defect of preventing men from realizing the extraordinary flexibility of the workings of history and the subtlety of the processes of time. Given the required intensity and intentness, a comparatively few Christians could alter the course of history as powerfully as the communists have done; and in fact this has already happened. It happened through the acquisition of power at a certain point in the story, however; and the power takes a terrible revenge on both the communism and the Christianity that lay hold on it. It might be said that the best Christian influence has always worked in history in a less spectacular manner, and has therefore had less tendency to provoke those counterbalancing evils which are responsible for the seamy side of the story. The profoundest effects on our civilization have been produced by people who were not thinking of affecting the course of human affairs at the mundane level; they have come as the unanticipated by-products of lives that had really been intent on spiritual things. The highest achievement is not that which takes the world by storm after the manner of modern communism; but that which, quietly penetrating free minds, acts as the leaven which leavens the whole lump.

It might be thought, therefore, that the Christian should withdraw from the tumult of international affairs, the whole sorry story of power, diplomacy, armaments, and war; and should even require of his country the same policy of non-co-operation. But those who disarm when a colossus like Russia maintains its forces are handing the world over to power, and may be permitting the extension of the area of conquest, violence, and suffering; for there is in Christianity no promise that a miracle will prevent a Russia from making use of her advantage in such an eventuality as this. If an individual consents to make a self-sacrifice—even to face martyrdom before a foreign invader—it is not clear that he has a socially recognizable right to offer the same sacrifice on behalf of all his fellow-citizens, or to impose such self-abnegation on the rest of his society. Certainly we can rejoice in one truth: there is something so impressive in the power which gentleness can have in the long run, that passive suffering and the willingness to be a martyr seem ultimately to move the world more than the resolution which meets force with force. And in the worst crisis, if renewed war breeds more wars, and civilization disappears in a thousand local conflicts, a state of misery could conceivably be reached in which the protest and the voluntary suffering of the pacifist might be the only lantern for the re-discovery of even the things which we call human values; provided the pacifism were consistent in its simplicity of mind—not the sort which can accompany over-vigorous action in the economic struggle for existence—not the sort which tries to dominate society by the formation of pressure groups. Wherever this form of witness authentically emerges, therefore, I presume that Christians would protect it in vindication of conscience, and guard it as the kind of treasure which keeps its value when all prudential calculations fail.

But at the present moment vast accumulations of military force—colossal slabs of power—are actually in existence all around us. Let us not close our eyes to this fact, any more than students close their eyes to the workings of cupidity in economic life. We may say that the power would dissolve, as mountains of ice dissolve away in the sun, if all men were to become Christian saints; but Christians, besides working for remoter purposes, have to look for those intermediate measures of relief which the condition of the world requires in the meantime. We cannot say that power would melt away if the world became formally and officially Christian after the manner of former ages; for, fifteen hundred years of Christian predominance in Europe failed to stop wars, failed to eliminate this problem of power. All we can ask —while the military force heaps itself up around us—is the question: Can the world be made more tolerable in spite of this power which solidifies in great masses amongst nations and empires? Since the power does not disappear merely because we wish it away or because we cry out that it ought not to be there, is there anything in our way of thinking about it which can mitigate its effectiveness or limit its role in history? We need not attach ourselves to anything which has been thought or attempted in the past; but if our predecessors found ways of moderating power or cushioning its effects, we must not feel that all these are to be swept away by a brush of the hand— there is a wisdom of former ages the cream of which, at least, is often capable of being transposed into modern terms. And if predecessors of ours had particular success in the establishment of a comparative stability in their world, and at the same time saw that a genuine international order required the maintenance of certain delicate conditions, their statements are not to be dismissed with a mere catchword about the dead past—especially by a generation which has so palpably failed in this respect. Above all, if the conclusions at which we arrive are more conformable to Christianity itself—more consistent with charity, more exacting in self-discipline, and more conducive to a Christian spirit even in time of war —than the ideas of the contemporary world; and if, to boot, they offer a foothold for a more scientific thinking, a more systematic reflection on such of our conditioning circumstances as might be amenable to intellectual control—then, to judge by analogous cases, we have found a point where Christianity can get a purchase on human history, and can insert the influences which have worked to the same effect in other fields. Only after the last armed State has dismissed the last army—if even then— will it be anachronistic to discuss this ever-present issue, or prudent to allow the matter to fall into neglect.

TWO

THE LIMITS OF A WAR OF DEFENCE

WHEN we look back upon the events of the last half-century, we can hardly avoid the impression that before 1914 our fathers were screened against the most fearful of the perils with which the world is liable to be confronted. At that time the three most momentous threats to the present-day order of things in Europe were either unimaginable or too remote to make an impression on the consciousness of Western man. It was possible to conduct one's thinking without remembering that in fact these three very things ought always to be regarded as at least a latent threat to an ordered society. So one forgot that the world is not naturally urbane, and that beneath all our civilizations the volcano rumbles in its sleep. It is since 1914 that we have come to see total warfare as a permanent threat to us, allowing of no relaxation in the foreseeable future. It is since 1914 that one form of revolution after another has come to menace our whole scheme of existence—revolution which, irrespective of the particular order that it attempts to impose, destroys just those things which need time and peace and historical continuity to bring them to their blossoming. Above all, nothing would have shocked the pre-1914 world so much as to encounter the third of our present-day evils—namely, the spectacle of what we call modern barbarism. The Edwardians knew that there were strange violences in the Balkans, where civilization still limped slowly in the wake of the receding Turk. But that highly-developed countries like Germany, Austria and Italy should become Balkanized, and should relapse into cruelties, despotisms, and sinister purposes—that peoples like ourselves should plunge back into forms of generalized barbarism—this hardly entered the imagination of the disciples of the idea of progress forty years ago.

All the three evils that have been mentioned are clearly the products of the same original evil. In each case the new menace goes back to that dismal birthday of modern battle and hatred, the War of 1914. The emergence of communism as a formidable force in the world; the birth of Fascism and Nazism and other parallel systems; the generation of resentments more profound and menacing than had previously existed; the Second World War itself and the rise of Russia to greater continental predominance than Germany ever enjoyed during the whole of her history; and, finally, the present enduring condition of war strain—all these represent lines of tendency in European history which arise out of the conditions produced by the War of 1914. It is remarkable to what a degree the communist revolution itself in the twentieth century has proved to be the very child of war.

Furthermore, it is true to say that the three evils we are discussing are not the result of the mere fact that war broke out in 1914. They spring rather from the protracted and desperate nature of that conflict—from the fact that war on this occasion was carried to the point where an established order is overthrown. Most unfortunate of all was the destruction of certain subtle assets, certain 'imponderables', which belong to an accepted 'international order'; for, as we shall see, where these are lacking, the fate of nations is liable to be more exposed to the play of naked force. It is claimed sometimes that, once hostilities have actually broken out, it is foolish in these days to imagine that a conflict can be restrained— foolish to dream of a war for limited ends, a war for a controlled purpose. Here is the very kind of assertion which it is most incumbent upon us to re-examine; and in the case that we are discussing let us note that one of the answers to the assertion is a thing which stands before all men's eyes. At this very moment we ourselves are engaged in a controlled and restricted war, a war for limited purposes, in Korea. Within a few decades we have had to come back to that maligned policy of warfare for a contracted and clearly-defined end; and for many reasons one might say that we are pursuing this policy in a period and under conditions much less appropriate for the experiment than was the case in the year 1914. The belligerents in 1914 were not so radically sundered as Russia and the West are sundered at the present day, but were still recognized as partners in an international order, members so to speak of the same club. Those were the conditions which made limited warfare a possible policy, and the urgent motive for such a policy was the maintenance of just those conditions, the preservation of the international order itself. Limited warfare was bound to be a less feasible policy in the after-period (in 1939 for example), when the further consequences of that mistake were being worked out.

As we see a broken Russia taking her fateful course in 1917—see how directly the merciless continuation of the war served the cause of the Bolsheviks in the climax of that revolutionary year—as also we see the coming of the landslide in East-Central Europe, and watch that great problem-area slipping out of the control of continental statesmanship—we must wonder what would have happened if all the leaders of the civilized world had had something of the attitude which they now seem to adopt in respect of Korea: the attitude which sees war itself as only the servant of a negotiated peace. And some of us must recall how even certain masters of *Real-politik* in the past, a man like Richelieu, for example, could make it a maxim not to allow the efforts of diplomacy ever to cease in time of war. The struggle which began in 1914, however, was fought on a basis that was bound to give the maximum scope to the hysterias and frenzies associated with the fury of battle. Precisely because it was conducted as a war 'for righteousness', a war 'for the destruction of the wicked', that whole conflict was turned into one that could admit of no compromise. Precisely because of the myth of 'the war to end all war', we made it more true than it had been for centuries that war breeds war, provokes revolution, generates new causes of conflict, deepens resentments, and produces those reversions which we call modern barbarism. The decision to fight an unlimited war, for the vindication of morality as such, amounted to a decision to give war a greatly enhanced role in history, but it did not alter the dreadful character of the role which warfare always plays. And since we cannot yet say that we have produced a world in which the possibility of war is at all ruled out, it is a question whether a more terrible moral responsibility does not lie upon those who insist on war *à outrance* than on those who had perhaps only the marginal responsibility for the outbreak of hostilities in the first place.

If the technical necessities of war may make peace impossible when the minds of people are most disposed to end the carnage, no one can deny that here the issue is quite a separate one; though many of the assertions that easily pass into currency even on this matter would also deserve a serious re-examination. What we are concerned with is the general attitude to war, to the moral issues it presents, and, most of all, to the objectives which are held before a nation; for once the unquenchable hatreds have been generated, the politician is quick enough to argue that it is public opinion itself which makes it impossible for him to end the conflict. Churchmen are concerned in

this; for it is too terrible a paradox if the Christian message
is so perverted as to add strength to a theory of war which
implies 'no peace by negotiation', insists on 'total surrender' and demands 'the annihilation of the wicked'.
Considerable fuel would be supplied for this unlimited
'war for righteousness' if the attention of churchmen were
concentrated on the condemnation of the sins of the
national enemy—or the potential enemy—at a given
moment (a condemnation which any time-server might
give without any strain on his moral courage); while the
soft pedal were put on the sins of our allies (so long as
they were our allies), and too great tactical agility
were employed to avoid the real test of moral courage:
namely, the exposure and the condemnation of our own
sins as a nation and an empire. As the raising of moral
indignation against a foreign people is the essential factor
in the fuelling of a totalitarian war, I wish I could be
more sure than I am that the churches of the various
nations—and particularly the Protestant ones, which are
exceptionally vulnerable in this respect—had pursued in
the cause of morality, what I should call the 'heroic'
path, which in the last hundred years individual Christians, individual atheists, and individual Marxists have
sometimes followed in a most moving manner. I need not
say that no national government could ever secure a more
powerful organ of official propaganda than a church
quickening moral indignation against the enemy of the
moment, and doing it on information which it fails to
test, information which, as the crisis deepens, is more
definitely controlled, more carefully filtered out to the
country, by the agencies of the home government itself.

During two thousand years the ecclesiastical mind in
general has tended to be particularly unfortunate in its
handling of historical data; for it has cherished more
legends than anybody else, has believed them longer than

anybody else, and has attempted to maintain them by force when all argument in their favour has lost its efficacy. It is a happy distinction which the Roman Catholic Church makes, therefore, when it contrasts the Pope's infallibility in respect of faith and morals with the possibility of his falling into error on historical matters. The Pope may put forward a principle that will guide one's judgement in regard to a case of aggression; but if he pretends to designate the actual aggressor it is always possible for Catholics to take the line that he has been misinformed. One of the items in the Christian tradition that has been handed down to us is the maxim that a Christian is justified even in resort to war, if he fights in self-defence, and *a fortiori* if he fights to defend the weak. We are not bound hand and foot by tradition, but we can hardly ignore this judgement; though it does not mean that a man or any body of men need regard it as a duty to resort to self-defence when they prefer to submit; and the Gospels point to a higher good which men can achieve even by turning the other cheek. There was one occasion on the eve of the Abyssinian War when the Pope made reference to this tradition and offered a commentary which is relevant to our present discussion. He put forward the significant general thesis: 'A war of defence is justified; but even a war of defence can be pushed too far.' To any dispassionate person the least that this thesis must mean is that, though your enemy may have attacked you first, and you have a right to defend yourself, his sin does not itself justify you in becoming an aggressor at his expense—does not justify you in carrying on the war for the purpose of destroying that enemy or breaking him up. There was a famous case in the eighteenth century of what was called 'a defensive treaty with an offensive *arrière-pensée*'. It amounted to the agreement: 'We will wait until Prussia attacks, but once she has given us the pretext for war, we will combine not merely for defence but for her radical dismemberment.' Such a policy, besides being ethically dubious in itself, is calculated to be harmful most of all (as we shall see) because it is precisely the method by which to destroy the international order. When France had taken part in what was intended to be a war of destruction against Prussia in the eighteenth century, some of her abler diplomats saw reason later for congratulating themselves on the defeat of that purpose, since they came to realize that the reduction of Prussia would have left them with more serious problems still.

The question whether the invasion of South Korea justifies the return invasion of North Korea raises one aspect of this whole issue, this problem of how far a defensive war may wisely or justifiably be carried. Possibly also the Austrian invasion of Servia in July 1914 would be worthy of reconsideration from this point of view. The least we can say is that the power which begins hostilities is not necessarily so wicked that it ought to be wiped out as a power. And, though Abyssinia was sufficiently responsible as a state to be admitted to membership of the League of Nations, we should hardly consider that Mussolini was justified in a war of total reduction, even if we granted that her tribesmen had actually been the offenders who had broken the peace on the frontiers. If it is argued that, once there has been an aggression, it is not sufficient to defeat its object and rescue the offended party, since the attacker will be able to renew the offence, this thesis is itself one of those which need careful re-examination. Sometimes, on the contrary, it is the creation of a new resentment which is more likely to be the provocation to new aggressiveness. Sometimes it is the demand for re-doubled security which is the more ruthless plan of aggrandizement and the cause of more desperate warfare. Bismarck was clearly justified when he said that he would intervene in an Austro-Russian conflict if it seemed that Austria, besides losing in the Balkan competition, was actually to be broken as a power. We are clearly justified if we say that we will join to save a Czechoslovakia or a Poland or a Russia from an attack on the part of a domineering Germany. We must not assume that we are necessarily justified if we re-define our professed object and set out to wage a war for the actual destruction of any state.

It will be seen later that the creation of an international order ought to be regarded—to say the least—in the way we should regard a proposal by a group of powers to erect a parallel to the British Commonwealth of Nations. We all know that we should demonstrate to these powers how such a thing is not made, but must grow—how a paper organization and the mere copying of our institutions represent the least important aspect of the matter; since it is only much profounder historical processes which can release the imponderable factors that it is part of our purpose to study—imponderable factors which we know are an essential part of the working of our Common-wealth. A purely formal international system—a mere skeleton of institutions—shares the weaknesses of a revolutionary régime, precisely because it lacks the assistance of these imponderables. In other words, an international system is precarious if its only sanction is force, and depends on the combined power of a temporary or permanent majority—it is weak, for example, if it can operate only by threatening the offender with the atomic bomb. Recalcitrant states may make minor encroach-ments or commit indirect offences in all parts of the world; and an international organ will not always feel that it is

justified in resorting to the atomic bomb. We are indeed
discovering that in a world so profoundly uprooted—with
many more regions dislocated and open to aggression than
in 1914—the *reductio ad absurdum* has been reached and
the whole mighty engine of a 'war for righteousness'
cannot be released every time.

So, by a grand culminating paradox, it is our international system—it is U.N.O. itself—which has returned
to flexibility, whether through wisdom or bad conscience,
or lack of power, or fear that public opinion could not
bear another world war so soon. Taking advantage of the
technicalities of the case (but certainly not moved merely
by the technicalities), it has returned to that warfare-for-
limited-purposes which has been so despised since 1914;
attempting in Korea to rectify a local evil without seeking
this time the destruction of either the power or the system
which it regards as morally responsible for the aggression.
All this is not because the guilty party is more innocent
or innocuous or unprovoked than Austria-Hungary in her
attack on Servia in 1914; but rather if anything in the
knowledge that the powers are now confronted with a
colossus more formidable and dangerous than ever. The
craziest partisan of the doctrine of limited war would have
been inclined to say beforehand that here was the most
paradoxical moment in all history for trying such an
experiment; though it would be difficult to avoid the firm
principle that if there is to be war the Christian must
insist that it shall be war for limited purposes. The
experiment is being carried out under conditions far less
favourable to it than in 1914, far less favourable to it than
at any moment since the rise of our nation-states. It is
we ourselves who have made it more difficult by our wars
for unlimited purposes, wars for total surrender, wars for
Utopia, wars for righteousness; and particularly by the
tragedy of 1914, which was calculated even to rob us of

the option of limited warfare in 1939 or as long as that particular chapter of story continues.

It is, therefore, not unfitting that we should go back to the past and find the point at which we might pick up again the threads which once were ruthlessly cut; examining the bases of diplomacy, the structure of the international order, the heresy of the 'war for righteousness', the conditions of limited warfare, and the direction of those lines of development in the past which sometimes give half a hint of the road to the future. For, so long as war is in men's calculations or fears, it is difficult to see how the Christian could refuse to give his mind to the question of limiting its scope and controlling its consequences. And because so many of the factors in modern warfare are outside our control, it is necessary to discover whether there are not any mental ones that we can alter —whether the nature of modern war is not at least partly affected by our way of thinking about it. Somebody clearly imagines that there is an area which is controllable; for it is nonsense to suppose that the engines of propaganda would be set to work upon us, as they are (sometimes in a degrading manner), save to produce a calculated effect. And before the twentieth century, what Christian, what civilized man, would have deprecated the kind of thinking which conduces to moderation in the ends of war? Above all, no arguments drawn from the character of modern weapons or the severity of modern warfare can invalidate principles which have reference rather to the objectives of the belligerents—the ends they are proposing to achieve if ever they reach the point at which they have the power to carry out their purposes. It would be something if we could make clear to ourselves the intellectual consequences which follow from the plain recognition of the fact that, apart from defensive objects, war decides nothing save the possession of controverted territory; and it decides this by the operation of force, not by virtue of any right. We tend to overlook the whole universe of things about which we should think differently if we could convince ourselves that, apart from its defensive function, war can decide nothing in fact except a redistribution of power.

Taking an extreme case, which has not occurred in our time, let us imagine that one state has invaded the territory of another state, and after three weeks of fighting finds the forces so equally matched that it prefers to withdraw from the adventure. The powers conducting the 'defence' prefer, however, that forces so equally matched should fight for years so that the aggressor may be depleted of a province by way of punishment. It is necessary to make a genuine analysis of the phenomenon of aggression before we decide that the latter course is more ethical than a return after three weeks to the situation that existed before the war; especially as the territorial confiscation does not operate as punishment is presumed to do—since the loser feels the forfeiture as the penalty not of sin but of defeat. And in reality a new resentment is created, so that what has been produced is merely the promise of a further conflict even more fanatical than before. In a world where the general presumption had produced the expectation of a warfare for limited ends, it is likely that all parties—with less to lose in the case of defeat and less to gain in the case of victory—would be more ready to compromise or to forgive or to confess their sins and mistakes. And some of the better thinking on this subject once came near to the thesis that if at the end of a war one restored the former situation (attempting as far as possible to eliminate the effect of the war itself)—or if at most one secured only a marginal rectification—one would be doing the maximum to reduce the role of war in history and to recognize the tragic element in it, so that for all parties the prize in the lottery would be less tempting in future. The actual resistance to an aggressor, and the combination against him, need not of course be any the milder in such a case. But the elimination of the concealed offensive—'We will wait till the enemy takes an initial step, and then we will pounce on him and wipe out all scores in every corner of the map'—would take from war the very thing which gives it its desperate character. And it only needs one party—though, of course, it must be the successful party—to show that moderation in the moment of victory which is the only thing capable of producing a *détente*.

Many are hoping that the time will come when the cold war will prove to have been the real war, and that it will not end by submerging itself in a totalitarian struggle for existence. These are the supporters of a war for limited purposes, even if they do not recognize the fact; and they at least may find something relevant to learn from the attempt which men once made to answer the question: 'In a world where we cannot eliminate war, how can we control it, and how can we maintain an international order still?' They will find that in diplomacy (as also in politics, when party bitterness has reached a maximum) there is no rescue for mundane systems themselves unless men will consider what is best for the world, even if it entails forgiveness of sins. Supposing it were to be claimed that much artificial bitterness must be manufactured in order to induce democracies to continue a war long enough even to achieve its defensive objects, it is still necessary that we should take care with the outer framework of our intellectual system—our over-all views on the subject of war and peace—so that life does not continue to be poisoned after the war is over.

THREE

THE 'WAR FOR RIGHTEOUSNESS'

IT has been held by technicians of politics in recent times that democracies can only be keyed up to modern war— only brought to the necessary degree of fervour—provided they are whipped into moral indignation and heated to fanaticism by the thought that they are engaged in a 'war for righteousness'. Over twenty years ago, while Mussolini was in power, Professor Ferrero issued a caution against this practice, and showed how it was likely to become the favourite device of war-mongers. He may have assumed that only Fascist dictators would employ this type of stimulus, but it would appear that Fascists are just the people who can procure a belligerent atmosphere by other means. Supposing it were proper, however, to subordinate ethics to reason of state, as such a policy requires, the consequences of the practice become serious when both parties to a conflict are made to see the struggle as a 'war for righteousness'. And the control of information and propaganda would make this a comparatively easy matter for a modern government; especially as sometimes a minor concealment or a trivial revelation can alter the colour of right or wrong in a particular affair. As, moreover, the 'war for righteousness' has actually been known in earlier periods of history, we are able to say that here is the clue to the deadliest features of modern war—the hatred, the viciousness, the refusal to compromise. The unlimited 'war for righteousness' was known centuries ago in fact; and we can learn from its terrible results at that time that it is this theory of war— and not modern scientific invention—which gives this kind of conflict its daemonic character. Indeed it is not sufficiently remembered how earnestly men once worked to escape the peculiar problems of the 'Wars of Religion', in which the conflict of right and wrong admitted of no relenting; and to what a degree it meant an over-all advance in civilization in our part of the world when it was possible to find a way out of the deadlock; with the result that later generations, looking back on that war-fare, regarded it as just the thing which must not be allowed to happen again.

It is not clear that this frenzy of the 'war for righteous-ness', this last extremity of moral indignation, is even tactically so necessary as the supporters of such a policy seem to imagine. Against the student of politics, the historian often holds the view that the passions of the masses, far from being difficult to arouse, are inconvenient precisely because they are so difficult to appease. And to most of us it is sufficient that we do not want the Russians or the Germans landing here and lording it over us, or endangering security by subduing their smaller neigh-bours. We should not want their eruption here or else-where even if we thought better of them than we do, or even if their leaders and soldiers were church-going Christians. We should be sufficiently angry with them for attempting the coup even if we were aware in our heart-of-hearts that, granted we were in the same position, we should be doing the same thing ourselves. We do not need to be told—as we were told in 1914—that our enemy is worse than the rest of human nature and that his wicked-ness demands utter destruction (so that all the resources of hyperbole are used up before ever a Hitler or a Stalin has emerged). And if there must be wars, it is good that the motive or the motor behind them should be the kind of purpose which is capable of dwindling in intensity as it achieves itself—dwindling as the war ceases to have some relation to self-defence, or to the defence of the country that is being rescued.

For one of the troubles of war is that it acquires its own momentum and plants its own ideals on our shoulders, so that we are carried far away from the purposes with which we began—carried indeed sometimes to greater acts of spoliation than the ones which had provoked our original entry into the war. Before the War of 1914 had lasted a year, its own workings had generated such a mood that we had promised Russia Constantinople and had bought the alliance of Italy with offers of booty, some of which had later to be disavowed by President Wilson. And it is a remarkable fact that in wars which purport to be so ethical that the states attached to neutrality are sometimes regarded as guilty of a dereliction of duty, the great powers primarily concerned may have required an iniquitous degree of bribery to bring them into the conflict, or to maintain their fidelity. The whole ideal of moderate peace aims, and the whole policy of making war the servant (instead of the master) of negotiation, is impossible—and the whole technique of the 'war for righteousness' has a particularly sinister application—when even in the ostensibly 'defending' party there is a latent and concealed aggressiveness of colossal scope, as there certainly was in 1914. And we have only to look at the case of Constantinople to realize that all pretended ethical explanations fall to the ground; for the Russians had feared lest the Turks should cheat them of their objective by failing to enter the war against them; while published commentary in Europe in the months before the crisis of 1914 show that their determination to have the city was then already a matter of notoriety. The long series of published selections from our Foreign Office documents shows a significant gap for the years 1914-19; and indeed the tales of cupidity in that period are a sufficient exposure of the tendencies of the 'war for righteousness'. In regard to the expropriation of the German colonies—and even bearing in mind the moral pretext upon which it was carried out—it may surprise many people to learn that for long periods in modern history both statesmen and writers, in respect of such a decision, would have swiftly and automatically objected: 'But this is being a judge in one's own cause.' And, once again, the cupidities which were involved in the transaction showed that the judges intended to gain profit from the sentence passed. Even the number of the judges does not matter, since they were victor-parties, all gaining some benefit from the general share-out. For, as somebody has said, if it had been the British Empire which had been in distress the number of vultures would have been at least as great, and they would soon have discovered a moral pretext for spoliation. One of the things Sir Edward Grey had been afraid of before 1914 had been some such general combination as this at the expense of the British Empire. To be sure, we should have been unwise to go to war with Germany at all if she had been no danger; and we should have been wicked if she had committed no offence. But in view of the crimes, sinister movements and aggressions of Tsarist Russia in the years before 1914, the pillorying of Germany as the sole wicked power in Europe—or even as so darkly wicked as Russia herself—deserves to stand on record for a long time as the slickest ethical conjuring trick in the whole of modern history.

George Kennan, in his book on *American Diplomacy, 1900-1950,* describes the pressures and moral indignations which led to the outbreak of war between the United States and Spain on the subject of Cuba in 1898; but he also notes how Theodore Roosevelt had long been wanting the Philippines, 'regardless of the circumstances of the origin or the purpose of the war'. He records how in the general hysteria, the islands appear to have been acquired 'on the basis of a very able and quiet intrigue by a few strategically placed persons in Washington'. The illustration shows how, by reason of the frenzy and hatred which have been aroused, the 'war for righteousness' extends the purpose of a conflict, and carries one's objective far beyond the immediate issue which had caused the outbreak of hostilities. Furthermore, all nations have their core of intriguers and masters of *Real-politik*, and by quoting these people alone—ignoring their proportionate weight in the country as a whole, and sliding over the question whether their ambitions are the decisions of the actual government —it is possible to show up many states as would-be aggressors, a technique which has been carried to great lengths by the enemies of Germany. The trouble is that these are the very people who tend to gain undue leverage the moment war actually breaks out, and they draw all the benefit that anybody ever draws from the heightened conception of war, and the hatreds that are generated. The implications of the 'war for righteousness' are that compromise becomes impossible, the original defensive object is superseded, the war becomes a war of unlimited ends, and—since there are only certain things that can be achieved by force—the root of the matter is: unlimited expropriation. It is not always remembered that this creation of 'irredentisms' is possibly the most potent of all the causes of future wars. We can hardly envy the lot of most of the populations that changed hands in 1919.

Indeed, if all wars are wars of unlimited ends—wars to end war, absolute conflicts of right versus wrong, and crusades against the supposed final seat of evil in the world—it does not at all follow that the outbreaks will be reduced in number or that the combats will be less intense. It merely means that we have given war itself a greatly magnified role in history and in the processes of time. More may be lost, but more also may be gained by a resort to arms, and the gamble is more momentous for those who are parties to the game; but the effect is not any the more deterrent to aggressors who generally feel that at any rate they have made success a complete certainty *this* time. Nor—as we can see—has the policy had the effect of making men and governments more virtuous when they reach a position in which they are able to act with impunity. Again, the converse is the case: for it appears that if you pillory John Smith as a scoundrel and send him to Coventry, the most sickening of the consequences is the likelihood that you will be able to make your own verdict come true. And if it was desired not to provide an opening for a Hitler in 1933, it would have been prudent not to have treated the Kaiser as though he had been exactly like a Nazi criminal in 1914.

The questionable character and the moral dangers of the 'war for righteousness' are still more clear to us if we face the fact that it is generally almost impossible for the most critical minds in any country to escape from that framework of story—both the details and the interpretations—in which a government formulates its case before public opinion. The problem and the predicament are not without their anguish when it transpires that great numbers of earnest Christians amongst the populations of the countries at war can be induced to feel in all sincerity that their nation is the injured one, and that their cause is the cause of righteousness. In 1914 theologians and churchmen on both sides felt that their country was fighting unwillingly for its very existence; and in the German case they acted sincerely on the information that was available to them—even Social Democrats, who would have been glad to catch the Kaiser out, were similarly convinced of their country's innocence. It came to be argued that the theologians of Germany were particularly gullible—reprehensibly eager to swallow the propaganda of their government. But there is not the slightest doubt that the British churchmen were in exactly the same case. Even the people who persist in anti-German polemics at the present day are forced to revise the original charges —forced to abandon myths on which our indignation was based in 1914. The German demand in 1919 that a body of neutral historians should make an impartial inquiry into the origins of the war was refused, as was only to be expected. But it is even true that governments themselves have no access to the inner minds of the foreigners with whom they are in conflict—they may not know at a given time the kind of considerations upon which a foreign power takes the course of action it does take. The story of the origins of the First World War is not even what the British Foreign Office thought it was in 1914, or in 1919; and this is often liable to be the case.

In this connexion there are other considerations of which we should take note, not in a querulous manner, but in the consciousness that they show what the world is like—possibly in the conviction that if they apply to England they will apply *a fortiori* to other countries. In diplomatic crises it is almost inevitable that much should depend on the way in which governments permit the facts of the case to be filtered down to the general public. Many people will remember no doubt the tremendous shock which Hitler's invasion of Norway in 1940 gave to one's moral susceptibilities. A pupil of mine, who had been one of the most authentic of conscientious objectors, and had been exempted from military service, was so appalled by the attack that his whole attitude was shaken, and he died not very much later in naval service. I have wondered sometimes what his reaction would have been if he had lived to know that Great Britain had had the prior intention of invading Norway—and this even irrespective of the desire to help Finland—and that Hitler, initially unwilling to undertake the adventure, had decided to forestall us. It makes a considerable difference if the real truth is allowed to leak out only at a later time, when all passion is spent and the senses have become numb. In the trial of the war-criminals, Admiral Raeder was charged (amongst other things) with his share in the German invasion of Norway; but he was not allowed to use in his defence the evidence relating to the British preparations which had been proceeding earlier still. We all realize that the law is what the lawyers say it is; but for the Christian it might be thought proper to wonder what the voice of morality has to say about such a matter.

Englishmen would be right in feeling that certain supplementary benefits which they draw from their society authorize in them an extra love of country, and a redundancy of harmless pride. Not the least of their advantages are the degree to which they enjoy freedom of speech, and the civilized manner in which control is exercised when it is necessary to restrict information, steer public opinion, or secure that the truth shall be filtered out in a desirable way in a time of crisis. It would be wrong for us to shut our eyes to the fact that, possibly rather by the operation of favour than by actual fear, a certain control is in reality exercised, however, and is particularly easy for a Foreign Office. Only in the year 1952, a question in the House of Commons resulted in the exposure of the fact that a mere hint from a High Commissioner had been sufficient to induce our newspapers to make a significant suppression of information. A frank protest on the part of a leader-writer in the *Daily Mail* on this occasion not only exposed the machinery by which control is made effective for practical purposes, but incidentally provided material for the unquestionable conclusion that the system is not voluntarily accepted by the Press, but is suffered in view of the sanctions that can be brought into operation. The events preceding the abdication of Edward VIII, when foreign newspapers were making revelations on matters concerning which the English Press was keeping so wonderful a silence, are evidence of the large-scale manner in which this whole form of what we might call "induced self-censorship" can operate on a national issue. Can it seriously be supposed that foreign affairs—concerning which we are supremely dependent for our information on official releases—are the single field in which the system is a negligible matter? In 1949 there was published in the United States a remarkable revelation of the scandalous manner in which the War Trial of General Yamashita had been conducted by the Americans. The book created a considerable sensation at the time, but the Japanese Press (after one paper had issued a notice) obeyed an American injunction to make no mention of it. If it is true that the book attracted no notice here, one cannot absolutely exclude the reflection that sometimes a subtle and possibly unconscious and probably unlocatable soft-pedalling is liable to occur, even in a country so free as ours, when an inconvenient truth has been brought to light.

It might be argued that all this represents a necessary discipline which government and society must exert if the affairs of a country are to be carried on at all. And we, who have so many reasons for happiness, will not querulously protest in a world where it is clear that much responsibility has to be confided to governments. Let us face the fact, however, that all peoples—and other nations more than our own, very often—are at the mercy of government officials, who have the defects of human nature. All that we have been noting is not a reason why a nation should not follow the direction of its government in the origin or the conduct of a war; but it gives us ample ground for saying that in general—in 1914, for example— we lack that information which might authorize us (if any information ever could authorize such a thing) to extend the implications of the conflict beyond the realm of limited political necessities—in other words, to carry the war against men's souls. In reality men are not granted the right to differ from their governments on the issue of a 'war for righteousness'. In the case of a war with Russia we should not permit the English communist to have the option of supporting the cause he thinks right. In any event, the hysterias of the 'war for righteousness' make nations less disposed than ever to allow a dissident view of what righteousness is. It might therefore be more con- ducive to honesty and clear thinking if we merely recog- nized that men have the duty to fight for their country and are in general left with no choice about the matter. In reality, they have both the duty and the inclination in ordinary circumstances; and if at a given moment they are ruled by a man whom they once supported for reasons of home policy, but who turns out wilful in foreign affairs—still it is hard for them to see why they should not try to resist the foreigners who are wanting to invade their hearths and homes. Nor are they likely to be reconciled to seeing their territory depleted in the time of their children and throughout an indefinite future unless the crimes of their government are more clear than they were in the case of Germany in 1914. Once it is possible to regard warfare as a thing which is undertaken for limited purposes, it becomes more easy to do justice to the plain truth that men are in fact prepared to fight for their countries and their homes.

Above all, there is a consideration which cuts at the roots of the 'war for righteousness', and that is the extra- ordinary intricacy and the terrrible fluidity of the political morality upon which nations base their judgements. We may add also the incredible inconsistencies which are open to governments through a quiet shifting of ground, and a subtle switching of ethical standards. If the Germans had held Persian oil, and we, looking on the controversy from the outside, had had to make a decision about the case, who can doubt that we should have brushed aside the mere question of law, or said that the Germans had taken advantage of an undue superiority in negotiation at a certain moment? Who could doubt that we should have appealed to morality itself, or possibly not even to morality, but to the vague horror raised by the question: 'What are the Germans doing, making an exploitation of another country's resources?' The discrepancy between the legalistic and the moralistic form of argument is itself sufficient to open a wide world for all the forms of war-mongering that could possibly exist. When George III fought the American colonies no person could have been more self-righteous than he, for on the legalistic argument the Americans were rebels, and here was a thesis that seemed to dispose of the whole issue. On this basis one could be moralistic and feel it one's duty not to relent, not to compromise in a conflict that must end in 'total surrender'. It could be argued that even if it had been wrong in the first place for the British government to attempt to tax the colonies, still, as a matter of principle, it was essential to hold out no conciliation to rebels while they were persisting in the act of rebellion. Yet there is a considerable body of English historical writing which condemns George III, and it makes great play with a resolute moral judgement which runs exactly to the opposite effect—it condemns George III and his war as tyrannical and reactionary. In the middle of the twentieth century the British government and people have not made their decision between the legalistic argument and the reference to first principles, to an ultimate standard of morality. We gain advantages from the privilege of sliding between the two; but our case is gravely exposed to attack from a formidable enemy or from the 'cad' who lays bare our inconsistencies. It is one of the weaknesses of public opinion—and of any merely oral treatment of such topics—that sides can quickly be taken in a quarrel on the strength of an apparently unanswerable thesis which covers a convenient selection from the facts of the case. The public shuns the baffling complexities which emerge when one tries to see all around a given problem, and to bring all the various types of consideration into one's survey. Hence the colossal opportunities which governments possess for imposing upon their peoples all the psychology of the 'war for righteousness'. It is not too much to say that the tragedy of the twentieth century is constructed on the basis of this very fact.

The identical phenomenon appears—and the evil gains added leverage—when the 'war for righteousness' generates its attendant form of popular historiography. And if we put a discipline upon ourselves we can always recognize this kind of history—always distinguish between the partisan and the student who is attempting to bring all factors into his survey. But the booby-traps themselves are not always discoverable even by the initiated, and topics could be mentioned by the score which would bring the matter home to any person who has experienced the propaganda of our generation. When told that Germany three times within a century (or four times within a century and a quarter) had invaded France, who would remember that the first occasion was when England and Russia had finally induced the German powers to join them in the effort to roll back the Napoleonic empire which had brought them low? Who would remember that on the second occasion the French, in an aggressive period during which they had cast their eyes on Belgium and Luxembourg, as well as on territory which had been German for over a thousand years, had made it clear that if they had won the War of 1870 they had determined upon aggrandizement much more scandalous than that of Bismarck himself? Who amongst the propagandists made it clear to the British public that even the story of Alsace-Lorraine did not begin with the crime of 1871, and that here was another of those terrible irredentisms—here was one of the regions where the aggressions of Louis XIV had most affronted the world? Who cautioned the British public that down to the time of the War of 1870 even a neutral could say that the French had been invading Germany for three hundred years, and something must be done about it? And the deceptions or the optical illusions in this final thesis are not a fraction of those involved in the converse of it, with which this argument began. Multiply these instances by hundreds, and you possess the whole fabric of that kind of history which becomes the conventionally-accepted basis of reference for the propagandists, that kind of history in which apparently on occasion even a Foreign Office can bury its head. Those who are locked in such a system can feel a great shock when they confront the strangenesses of a German, or a Jesuit, or a Communist, or a Protestant version of European history. Yet in a sense they are all made out of the self-same recipe; and the same mathematical formula—the same principles of exclusion and selection—*mutatis mutandis* will account for the commonest type of aberration in all of them. The English, because they are unconscious of doing any work of interpreting—unconscious that there is anything to interpret—are particularly vulnerable at the present moment. Various significant pointers in the last thirty years make it clear that if events give Marxist history a chance to secure the ears of men, or to establish a foothold in the country, there is so much intellect as well as plausibility in its use of the general recipe that the English version would collapse like a house of cards. We cannot be saved from Marxist history unless we show more self-discipline and greater integrity even here.

It might seem to many people that, when the crimes of the enemy have been patent, the trial of individual culprits by the victor-powers is a fitting culmination to a 'war for righteousness', and a vindication of the principle of justice in the world. The matter has not been left unconsidered by our predecessors, who felt, however, that the structure of justice was gravely undermined when those who were parties to the conflict conducted the trials, so that the prosecutor was also the judge. In a world in which the suffering of millions is so great that even the suffering of an extra million could hardly stretch compassion more—in a world where also it seems necessary to hang a pitiful murderer whose case we should want to exempt if the safety of society permitted it—let it be clear that there can be no question of particular consideration for many of the victims of the trials which have actually taken place. What perturbed our predecessors was the possibility of abuse that the procedure concealed, and the fantastic degree to which the abuse was capable of being carried, especially as this is justice which is executed before the fever and the heat of battle are quite over. For there can be no question that if the righteous hang the wicked for their responsibilities in a war, the wicked, when they are victorious, will take at least an equivalent revenge on their enemies, and will make virtue of their attachment to justice and righteousness in the very act. But if wars are always to end—as total wars now will— in the execution of enemy statesmen, or of service-men who obeyed the orders of their government, the net result at the finish is only the addition of a new horror and a new desperateness to war. For the statesmen will compel their people to fight to further degrees of wilfulness in order to save themselves; and, if they commit still more shocking crimes for the purpose, what will that matter to them if they are to be hanged in any case? Precisely because the infliction of suffering is so terrible a thing, it is our duty to prevent or to stop it where we can act without adding to it; but it is not virtue to avenge if we open the gates to a further realm of suffering and atrocity. And Pharisaism exceeds itself when a man thinks that he is more attached to virtue because he wishes to punish or wishes even to double the punishment for sin—to inflict a capital penalty for the crime of robbery, for example. For the robber in such a case will only find it the more necessary to escape capture, and knows that they cannot do more than hang him even if he shoots a police-man. It was always possible to predict, therefore, to what point the trials of war-criminals might develop within the course of shall we say a century. But the case of General Yamashita demands serious consideration. For even a jealous critic would hardly have predicted that the evils would already have begun to appear in the first American war-trial that ever occurred.

FOUR

HUMAN NATURE AND HUMAN CULPABILITY

EVEN if our New Testament were a work of fiction, and were presented to us as the achievement of an imaginative poet, its disturbing challenges and its exposure of the human plight would still be as valid as ever they were, and as vivid as ever a Shakespeare could make them. And those who do not believe that a Jesus ever rose from the dead must recognize that somebody has left a pattern there, which has the effect of convicting every one of us.

It is staggering, however, to see the elementary character of the ideas which appear to prevail in the world on the subject of morality in general, and particularly on the question of human guilt and human culpability. Sometimes it would be less harmful if it was really believed that men are like automatic machines, the mere products of heredity and conditioning circumstance, so that sin would be only a disease or a maladjustment. The non-Christians do not adopt this attitude, however, at any rate when they are considering other people's sins. On the contrary, irreligious though they may be, they tend to be cruelly, grimly, appallingly, and even hideously moral, in a way that is calculated to be ruinous to the world. They tend to be moral in a manner that is actually stultifying; and indeed they are often not moral at all, but only moralistic. Just the thing that the pagans do not do is to make allowances for other people's sins, allowances for heredity and environment, for education and predicament, for favourable opportunities on the one hand and the constricting force of circumstances on the

other. They do not even make allowances for the sins
which they themselves would commit if they were in the
other person's place. Partly because it asserts the sinfulness of all men, Christianity, in its doctrine of Love, goes
beyond any other system in its recognition of all those
points in which it is the duty of human beings to make
allowances for one another. It goes further than any
other system in its vision of what there is which is worth
saving in every human creature; and though it brings a
consciousness of sin, it refuses to see any man as necessarily the slave of his own past. It does not encourage but
destroys what one might describe as that paralysing feeling of guilt which men sometimes desire to impose upon
a defeated enemy.

It is a paradox that the highest and most spiritual view
of life which is available to man—and the one which
carries human beings to the most elevated and rarefied
realms of experience—is one which starts with the assertion of universal human sinfulness. The very ladder which
has carried men to those exalted spheres and regions of
light has an end which rests in the mundane realm on the
primary recognition of this fact. The finest examples of
human sainthood and the finest blossomings of human
personality seem to emerge out of an initial abasement of
the human being before this very truth. They seem indeed
to be inseparable from a continuous confession of sin, and
the very power which works with such efficacy in holy
people is the knowledge of the forgiveness of sins. It is
hardly necessary to say that the recognition of all men as
sinners is calculated to have momentous effects upon the
whole world of human relations. It would be the Christian
assertion, I feel sure, that human relations can never be
properly envisaged—nor, of course, could any science of
them be possible—except after this situation has been
squarely faced. Even if we pictured Christians as set

against the rest of the world, we should say that the Christians were the confessed sinners, not that they were the righteous arrayed against the wicked. In any case, we should not take the line that ours was a warfare against the rest, but rather that it was warfare on their behalf. From the time of the Gospels, indeed, it is precisely the self-righteous who are the enemies of the spirit of Christ. And it is a pity that the modern world has lost so much of the moral teaching which is to be drawn from Christ's controversies with the Pharisees.

But the greatest menace to our civilization today is the conflict between giant organized systems of self-righteousness—each system only too delighted to find that the other is wicked—each only too glad that the sins give it the pretext for still deeper hatred and animosity. The effect of the whole situation is barbarizing, since both sides take the wickedness of the other as the pretext for insults, atrocities, and loathing; and each side feels that its own severities are not vicious at all, but simply punitive acts and laudable measures of judgement. In this connexion, let us note that if the world ever drops the notion of sin as a crime against God and replaces it by the notion of sin as a crime against man, we shall be setting civilization back by far over two thousand years, back to a date far earlier than the life of Christ. For the present-day world, as it makes this transition, is not only turning its back on Christ, but is turning its back on humanizing ideas about the nature of sin which can be traced to great religious movements in Asia hundreds of years earlier still. If man arrogates to himself the right which he is not fitted to possess, and which Christianity withholds from him—namely, the right to judge actual wickedness, to adjudicate on sinners and to punish the sin itself—then there can be no end to the atrocities. For man without God is terrible to those whom he chooses to regard as sinners; and he has become more terrible since he lost the idea of the Judgement of God, so that he dare not leave anything to the Judgement Day, for fear that this will never take place, and the sin will go for ever unpunished.

All this does not mean that Christians are to tolerate cruelty and suffering; for our endeavour in this respect has to stop short only at the limit of what is practicable or possible. It means rather that our endeavour to improve the world is not to be distracted or interrupted by considerations of justice that are purely of the vindictive kind. At this point, as at many others, the world is liable to overlook the strategic significance of the Christian principle of Love. When Francis Bacon urged the case for a new kind of knowledge which should be more capable of being harnessed to human utility, he used that Christian doctrine itself against what he regarded as mere intellectual indulgence on the part of the Aristotelians. On this basis he insisted upon the importance of a form of thinking which would relieve the lot of human beings. If, when all things are considered, we can diminish suffering, or can better train a child, by leaving an offence unpunished, then there is no blind judgement of heaven that will be warped to all eternity by our charitableness of mind. If we can win a man from a delinquency by treating him as no worse than other people, there is not an angry God who will say that He has been cheated in the winning of this soul. And the Christian, conscious of so many sins unpunished, is not the person who will insist on punishment when punishment is actually harmful. Nor will he fill the world with the uncomprehending resentments of men who—as in 1914—knew little of the crimes imputed to them, and indeed suffered chiefly perhaps because they were the heirs of the system of Bismarck. Above all, if we really wish to enter into the fundamentals of the case, we should note that the real challenge to human sin is the challenge which itself springs from love. The case for the moralities can never be met if the culprits are being pilloried merely by political enemies, and if communists are charged by Englishmen in a manner calculated to improve nobody's lot in Russia, and only to generate more malice here. There is a 'war for righteousness' in the universe, but it is not fought at the level at which it serves the militant needs of one state against another. Even ecclesiastical systems which have made manifest the virtues of charity, are sometimes shown up badly in history when, instead of winning men, they proudly condemn—now trouncing the vices of democratic leaders without mentioning the virtues; and now showing more fervour in condemning sins abroad than sins nearer at hand. Even the Church is only invincible when it denounces man's universal sin—that is to say when it brings my own sins home to me.

And, curiously enough, it is not clear that on a last analysis, the historian, commenting on the evils of our time, will judge that the real source of them was any unusual criminal—even a criminal like Hitler himself. Criminal natures are likely to be found in all countries, and a healthy, stable order of things is likely to keep them in their place. If a man like Hitler gained a position from which he had the power to do magnified harm, it is quite conceivable that he never could have reached it but for the minor sins and small delinquencies and petty lapses from duty on the part of multitudes of men—multitudes not merely in Germany, but in other countries. And these multitudes were men, who, indeed, may have had their wilful moments, but who never felt themselves to have been doing any great harm. And, similarly, if in one age aggression is more terrible and violent than in another age, that is not to be explained on the argument that human nature is being produced on the earth in baser forms now than ever before. It reflects a failure in respect of that whole system of safeguards which has to exist in times of stability—safeguards against the cupidity of states, preventing men from feeling that circumstances give them the opening for a high gamble or a colossal design. And when all the responsibilities are levelled out and properly distributed, even the shallowness of modern idealists and the egotisms of the system-makers are not likely to be exempt. Furthermore, all this explains why the historian, as time recedes, sees the emergence of a Napoleon or a Hitler as an historical process which can be scientifically analysed.

There are vast numbers of people who can be regarded as neither absolutely vicious nor utterly unselfish, neither criminals nor saints. And some show a fine face to the world while they live in a conventional society, and have a smooth going-on, with only small temptations, and no storms but storms in a tea-cup. Virtue in such cases is remarkably dependent on combinations of circumstances; and this must be one aspect of the Fall—namely, the fact that human conduct is so subject to conditions. Many will be reasonably virtuous if the conditions are not too hostile and the price is not too high; and things are so disposed that all the arrangements of a stable, healthy society tend to keep these people on the rails. Once there is a police strike, or a revolution, or a terrible dilemma, we are astonished to see how ugly this ordinary human nature can be; and it is then that we learn how greatly respectability had been buttressed by institutions.

These are the people—neither black nor white—who, when their nations are at war, will be passionately self-righteous, burning with indignation against one another. If the issue were plainly put before them they would shudder and shrink from the idea of dropping an atom-bomb at Hiroshima for the purpose of turning a negotiated peace into the luxury of 'total surrender'. But when such issues are presented to them—as they always are—somewhat muddied and complicated, they can see reason and right (observing the act from the point of view of the doer) in the very thing which would outrage them if it were done by the enemy and seen only from the outside. Alternatively, they can be sincerely horrified by an atrocity imputed to General Franco. But when the same atrocity is attributed to the Greek communists or to an ally of their own, they can be equally sincere in blotting out the culpability—blotting out everything from their minds save the allowances to be made, or the inner reasons which render the action more understandable.

Now it is the experience of history and the teaching of historical Christianity that something can be done even with this world of half-lights, this grey, drab universe of the half-righteous. And it is precisely because their conduct responds so greatly to conditions that we are able to have a science of society or a scientific history, and can show the processes of a revolution, or examine the development of a class-war, or estimate the probable reaction of public opinion to a given policy. It is against these people—against men like ourselves—that we raise up our mighty indignations when our country is at war. Yet the Christian attitude to them is not merely the higher charity; it is the only attitude that is consonant with a scientific treatment of human problems. Indeed, the great enemy in these human concerns—and particularly in the problems that relate to war—is the tendency to myth and eschatology. And the greatest advance was made in the treatment of the issue of war itself, in an age which rejected myth and eschatology at least in this particular branch of human affairs—an age which saw human nature as one, and was aware of its defects, but which, in these very defects, saw the grounds for a scientific attitude. For there could be no science of human affairs if all human beings were like gods, reigning unconditioned; or if there were no laws formulating the general effects of even ordinary egotism and wilfulness.

One of the greatest problems of the present day is the curious phenomenon which we have described as 'modern barbarism'. It is the kind of thing which, for understandable reasons, existed in the Balkans before 1914, and was long discernible even in the politics of that peninsula. It is the question of a kind of barbarism which can exist amid all the external apparatus of a civilized world; so that we may find it in countries which have suffered a reversion through wars, breakdowns, revolutions, disorders, or conditions of unusual pressure and desperation; but also we may find it in countries which have assimilated the science and technology, but not the subtler virtues of civilization—countries which have copied democratic institutions without realizing the tolerances and urbanities and self-discipline which they require. At the root of the whole phenomenon is a hiatus in the transmission of the higher values of a civilization, a defect in the way in which the traditions of a society have been handed down. Often it is the imponderable virtues of a culture which are allowed to evaporate unless men take care of them; so that what we are really dealing with is the case of 'the disinherited', the case of people who have been deprived of an essential portion of their legacy. We even know that partial manifestations of the phenomenon may appear in our own country, if, owing to a war, a younger generation is allowed to miss an essential part of the teaching that is due to it. The same effect might be produced if, owing to a materialism in our outlook, we were to allow a purely technical training to supersede the education in human relations and human values. Our own world still possesses much humanity in spite of its departure from faith; for it is full of men who are virtually lapsed Christians, soaked in the traditions of our religion and the ideals of the Renaissance. But even in our own world we can begin to see what happens when a legacy so distinct and clear as this begins to melt away in the ocean of materialism. We can measure in some of the countries of Europe, therefore, the relations between cause and effect in the phenomenon of modern barbarism, where the legacy of Christianity and the traditions of humanism have been violently dispersed.

Wherever modern barbarism emerges we find ourselves shocked to see one general consequence. It is the disappearance of the tolerances and urbanities and self-discipline which we associate with a civilized world. Occasionally we find in history that the transmission of these things to a new class of society—previously 'disinherited' also to a certain degree—may become of momentous importance at a time when there is a redistribution of power inside a given country. Behind the evils that we deplore lies the failure to respect the other man's personality, the absence of the process of looking inside the other man's mind—there is an impulsive way of deciding that the man who disagrees with one's views is a rogue or a fool or a vested interest. And in proportion as men have missed the training and the legacy which belong to the higher aspect of civilization, this failure in the respect for human personality seems to become the more complete in its barbarity, and it is the quality of mercy which withers from the world. And *ipso facto* all conflicts—even party conflicts within the State and even personal quarrels—take on the blind uncomprehending character of 'wars for righteousness'. Whether modern barbarism in its most brutalized and uncivilized form occurs in Germany or in Russia, in Palestine or in China, in revolutionized lands or in countries engaged in totalitarian war, the result is the same, and the thing which has been most horrifying in those cases is precisely the thing which they have had in common. We could almost provide the mathematical formula for the evil; for it reduces itself to contempt for the other man's personality, the belief that the enemy 'deserves' killing, the refusal to contemplate the case of the innocent thousands who may have suffered at Hiroshima. Those who can drive motors and move mountains and survey the stars, may still be capable of failing to imagine the case, failing to feel the suffering or to be moved to mercy. And the men who in the nineteenth century expressed misgivings concerning the future of democracies, feared just this phenomenon. They feared most of all that civilization would become submerged under those very 'wars for righteousness' which have been so disastrous in our time.

What is more, it is apparent that we cannot cure the evil merely by becoming like this ourselves, merely by falling into the same sins. That is one of the reasons why we have to beware of 'wars for righteousness' and beware of forming a counter-system to communism which must end by becoming all too like the system of communism itself. Special laws necessarily come into operation as soon as it is conceived that atrocity and cruelty are generalized, so that they represent a mass phenomenon; for once this has happened it means that something has gone wrong with the conditions of human life, and in a certain sense moral indignation is beside the point. It means that we cannot rectify the case by attacking the evil direct, but must address ourselves to the remedying of the conditions which produced the evil. In a similar way, special laws necessarily come into operation as soon as it is conceived that we are a civilized world which is now compelled to fight a type of barbarism; for at the root of barbarism there is something that is not disposed of by a moral judgement, and, though it may be necessary to be most competent in one's defensive measures, here is just the one great evil that can never be cured by mere punishment.

There was a time when Whigs and Tories thought equally badly of one another—in their great duel of Right *versus* Wrong. The executions procured by the one party when it was in the ascendant provoked the desire for reprisal in the other party when the situation was reversed. It would have been possible to go on indefinitely with such a conflict, and at every new turn of fortune the policy would have seemed more justifiable than before, since the enemy would have given more definite reason for punishment. In fact it is difficult to see any escape from such a circle unless somebody who has the power to inflict punishment choses to withhold it, though the enemy seems to deserve it more than ever. The English political tradition was produced in the very process by which English party politics came to be turned into a form of 'limited warfare'. It was produced by virtue of the Christian interpretation of righteousness and by means of those very procedures which it is our present purpose to examine after they have been transposed on to the scale of international conflict. England is indeed the happiest of all the illustrations of the fact that civilization itself requires the doctrine of the forgiveness of sins. And the pattern of this doctrine reproduces itself in incredible manifoldness in the very cells that go to make the fabric of an urbane and tolerant world.

FIVE

AGGRESSION

IF we go through four or five centuries of modern history, studying the successive cases where the extreme kind of aggressor has emerged, we find that the various nations of the continent have taken up the sinister role in turn, apparently pushing forward to what used to be called 'universal dominion'. There is Spain under Philip II in the sixteenth century; France under Louis XIV and then under Napoleon; Germany in the period of the two world wars; and, finally, in the present generation, Russia. It is curious to note that states which have been comparatively well behaved during the course of centuries—states which have hardly ceased playing an important part in the work of saving Europe from the domination of a great power—are often liable to emerge at the next stage of the story in the character of tyrants and aggressors. On each successive occasion the people who feel themselves imperilled think that the aggressor of the moment is the only power that ever was an aggressor; and over and over again, in the course of a long period, Englishmen described the French as 'the perpetual aggressors, the eternal enemy of the Continent'. When peoples are in this mood they refuse to think that any other power ever could be so ambitious, so wickedly intent on their subjugation. Most of all, they refuse to imagine that some other state, now their ally and friend, could ever change character completely and go over to so evil a role. So it has often been noted by historians that the English, who continued fighting so bitterly against the predominance of Spain in the seventeenth century, failed to see how they were helping the France of Louis XIV to become the next menace to the Continent. After the fall of Napoleon in 1815, it was the British in particular who insisted that Germany was too weak in relation to France, too weak to act as a barrier against aggression. We therefore determined to strengthen Germany's western frontier and give Prussia a strong establishment in the Rhineland; though Prussia was unwilling to accept this, partly because it was calculated (and was even intended) to bring her into conflict with France. In this way we actually helped the Germans to become the aggressors at the next stage of the story, and we provided a considerable addition to those factors which were to bring Prussia to the leadership of that country. After the Second World War, the very completeness of our victory, and the very thoroughness of the steps which we took to end the German menace, have only had the effect of leaving the power of Russia comparatively unchecked, and bringing the new danger much more close to our own doors.

It is still more curious to note that the historian would find it difficult sometimes to fix the moment when the various powers of Europe, turn by turn, actually did become aggressors. Even the powers themselves, even the statesmen concerned, could hardly tell when they passed from a defensive policy, and then a reasonable demand for 'securities', to a point where they made themselves the directors of a scheme of conquest. In the early days of Louis XIV's reign it could still be argued that the French frontier came dangerously near to Paris, so that a policy of aggrandizement was able to issue in a natural way out of considerations that had been originally defensive. Even when Bismarck took Alsace-Lorraine there was an American minister in Berlin, the historian Bancroft, who supported his policy, asserting that a rectification of frontier was necessary to guard the country against French attacks, which had been continually repeated for three hundred years. In any case, the whole map of Europe is honeycombed with areas of claim and counter-claim, areas that are the subject of irredentist aspirations, ethnical controversies, historical grievances, and nationalist demands. If a state becomes for any reason strong enough to assert its rights or to rectify some former abuse of power—strong enough to recover what it had once lost through weakness—it does not always actually feel itself to be an aggressor. It may only be conscious of protesting against established injustices such as the other powers (and even in recent decades the League of Nations itself) had often been prepared to leave untouched, out of regard for vested interests.

In all these respects—and having in mind the kind of evidence that has been summarized—it is irrelevant to say that the national character of one people is worse or more wicked than that of the others. The most remarkable feature of the kind of cases which are illustrated in this survey is the almost mechanical sameness and repetitiveness of the actions and reactions which the student of history observes. We may ask: 'What is it that makes a state, which has been comparatively virtuous for a long period, emerge at a given moment as an aggressor?' And it would not appear that the data before us, or any historical analysis, would support the view that the sinister change is the consequence of a certain type of political régime, or that the constitution of the government is by any means the most important factor in the case. It is not possible to say that liberal states or liberal parties are in any sense out of reach of the temptations involved. Much has been made recently of the militant annexationist dreams of the German liberals in 1848; but

even their ambitions are trivial compared with the course
of conquest adopted by the French Revolutionaries long
before Napoleon had been brought to power. We cannot
say that democracies are exempt; for if anything they
seem in history to have been more bellicose than kings,
who after all were generally related to one another—
more bellicose than aristocrats, who so often formed an
international fraternity, and at any rate understood one
another's language and mentality. It would even seem
to be the case that young democracies and new nations
are particularly prone to irredentisms, or dreams of
expansion, or enterprises of revenge, or projects of conquest.

One fact seems absolutely clear: namely, that revolutionary states are particularly aggressive, and this applies
to all kinds of revolutions, even to the democratic or the
religious or the communist sort. That is to say, the mere
fact of being a revolutionary state is the decisive point,
irrespective of the actual character of the revolutionary
creed involved. Even so, revolutionary governments
seem to continue, sometimes only with greater *élan* and
efficiency, the very lines of territorial aggrandizement
which had been marked out by their monarchical predecessors. Of this both the French and the Russian
revolutions have supplied us with some notable examples.
It is not clear that Soviet Russia has added anything
fundamental to the character of the revolutionary crusade
as it developed in 1792–93 at the time of the first French
Revolution. The same logic leads a missionary cause to
projects of universal dominion in both of these instances;
and the propaganda is identical when both revolutionary
systems incite foreign workers to refuse support to their
own government in a war against the new régime. Let
us add also that small states themselves—even those which
have had very recent experience of oppression and

have had to struggle hard for their own liberty—show
the same cupidities and aggressiveness when for a moment
they see a chance of catching a local opportunity. Even
amongst the city-states of Renaissance Italy the same
tendencies are apparent. Even Berne, a member of the
Swiss confederation, after freeing Geneva from the
Duke of Savoy in the early decades of the sixteenth century, could not resist the temptation of territorial conquest, and became in turn a danger to the liberty of
the Genevans themselves. And if we glance for a single
moment at either the history or the extent of that British
Empire on which the sun was supposed never to set, the
most fervent patriot amongst us will hardly dare to claim
that our own country has been in any sense an exception
to the rule.

Taken together, these points confirm the traditional
view that aggressiveness is somehow related to the
character of power itself. When Acton said that power
tends to corrupt and absolute power corrupts absolutely,
his thesis comprised this exact point: even if a state has
been virtuous hitherto, a certain position of power—
a position in which the state knows that it can act with
impunity—will in fact produce a corrupting effect. And
we can see enough in history to justify the assertion that
even if in the place of the word 'State' we put the word
'Church' (having in mind those visible ecclesiastical
organizations that play their part in mundane history) the
same principle holds good; for, even there, men will go
on simply expanding their power once they see that they
are in a position to do it with impunity. So we arrive at
the thesis put forward by Lord Acton towards the close
of the first of his *Lectures on Modern History*. Acton says
that there is one thing which has caused more strife in the
world than race or religion or the conflict of political
ideas; and that is the tendency of power as such to expand

indefinitely, transcending all barriers at home and abroad, until it is met by a force superior to it.

A purely moralistic attitude to aggression would assert that the offence is due to the emergence of an unusually wicked man or state, and there the matter would have to rest. It is tantamount to the case of the Pharisee who is proud and self-righteous because he is not like the wicked drunkard passing down the street; for in all this it is assumed that men make themselves and exert a will that is independent of conditions. The essential point, which the modern myth-makers evade, is the fact that the phenomenon in question is amenable to further analysis. The Christian who succeeds in avoiding Pharisaism is bound to inquire whether heredity or environment do not have some say in the matter, whether indeed God may not look with greater pity on the case of the drunkard, since the Pharisee may be the more responsible for having hardness of heart. And because the Christian attitude attributes to the frailty of man a less degree of sovereignty, a greater dependence on conditions, we can come to deal scientifically with the question of the conditions that make for juvenile crime, for example; or we can push out the frontiers of the science of psychology over psycho-analytical cases which former ages would have dismissed as diabolically evil. We do not eliminate human responsi-bility altogether, nor do we deny—on the contrary, we assert—the power of man to rise more and more above conditions. But if we did not recognize the relevance of a whole context of conditioning circumstances we should not be able to weave together the fabric of history at all—every action would be in a sense un-caused, and referable to nothing save the unconditioned will of the doer. In this sense the scientific treatment of these matters depends entirely on the adoption of the Christian rather than the Pharisaical attitude.

All this extends to the realms of politics and diplomacy, where, once we have found the foothold for a more scientific method, it is not easy to place limits to the distance to which it may be carried. For example, once we have seen that aggression is a thing which depends on conditions, we can try to discover whether, though it is so difficult to control the aggressor after he has actually appeared, we may not tackle the problem at a stage earlier—that is to say, by preventing the emergence of the conditions which make for aggression. It is not always realized that for a long period in European history it was assumed as a commonplace that all the guns of diplomacy should be trained upon an earlier stage of the whole problem. However difficult this may seem to be, it can never be so difficult as the task of dealing with the evils of predominant power after they have materialized—after the pistol has actually been pointed at us. It is at least more feasible to check the emergence of the conditions which make for an aggressor than to trust to the virtue of men at this earlier stage in the argument, and then have to deal with the aggressor after he has actually shown his hand. And if this is forgotten by a given generation, that generation will suffer from the evils of war more than its predecessors, not because men are born more wicked than before, but because they have overlooked one of the conditions of peace.

In other words, if Germany and Russia are both strong —or, alternatively, if both are weak—the fact that they stand in awe of one another will undoubtedly tend to moderate their aggressiveness. It is even possible that, after a long period of such stability, both of them will lose the habit of thinking about aggression; for this is one of

the ways in which the world improves itself. The same
conditions provide the maximum opportunity of happiness
and autonomy for all the smaller nations that lie in the
intermediate region. For this reason it is to the advantage
of the rest of Europe that neither of these giants should
ever be allowed to wipe out the power of the other even
for a decade; and it is legitimate to go to war to prevent
the destruction of a state, but not for the purpose of
completing its destruction. For, given that it possesses an
unreasonable ascendancy, the one will behave very much
like the other, whatever the régime—the extent of the
aggression almost proportioning itself mathematically to
the degree of predominance and impunity which either
of these giants obtains. And if it is argued that the wills
of men are free, and that a Stalin may prove virtuous after
all, still this is not a security in which one can confide,
especially if Stalin should count it a virtue to extend to a
wider world what he regards as the blessings of Marxism.
Granted that he is unusually righteous, it is necessary to
say to him that though we confide in his virtue we cannot
be sure about his successor; for power conceded to
Russia as a body politic cannot be withdrawn because we
dislike a new ruler who climbs later into the seat of
government. Furthermore, if Stalin is virtuous, he will
understand the argument, and realize that the world
cannot surrender its guarantees of security merely out of
regard for a man whom it trusts or a state which it
happens at the moment to like. We might even add that,
granted the acquisition of power, a Stalin might prove to
be virtuous, but in the new conditions might not be able
to keep his control in Russia itself. We might say that
even if the United States found itself master of the world,
it would become less likely that a man of reasonableness
and moderation would be elected to the Presidency.
In the course of a revolution, a leader who is too squeamish

E

is liable to be displaced; so that his freedom to choose his conduct does not alter our general views on the processes which a revolution undergoes. Similarly, the son of an industrial magnate may be too sensitive for the business world and may withdraw from it in order to give his life to music. As his place will be filled up by somebody else, his freedom of choice does not alter our general ideas about economic development or invalidate a science of economics.

All that we have been discussing leads to the further conclusion that we can study processes in history which lie deeper than the wills of men. These themselves do not eliminate human responsibility but they qualify the moral judgements that men are often so eager to make. It is necessary to qualify even the moral judgements that were made on Napoleon when we learn that, before he had emerged, the progression of the French Revolution to a military dictatorship had been predicted as unavoidable; and that before he had been adopted as a likely candidate the project of a *coup d'état* had been contemplated, with a different general as the chosen leader. And similarly we should trace the origin of the war of 1914 back to general processes and widely-distributed responsibilities which run through a period of fifty years; and as an illustration of the dispersion of responsibility that may result, we might consider the case of certain Belgian diplomats, who before the crisis of July 1914 were examining the drift towards war, and who put the responsibility not upon Germany at that time but on the aggressiveness which they had noted in the Entente.

This methodical handling of historical material is possible only when we abandon the initial attitude of the Pharisee and accept our own part in man's universal sin. And if we pursue this course we discern the deeper tragedy of human conflict, and

learn to have a greater compassion for all the human
race.

Finally, there are a number of ways in which we ourselves
may provoke aggression, or may so behave that we give
occasion for sin. As defenders of the existing order of
things, we may be committing a crime if we disdain
protests and appeals from states which at the moment are
not backed by power; though in this connexion it may
be noted that the sins of the defenders of the *status quo*
have a way of losing themselves, or hiding themselves,
in a conjuror's hat. One fault of our crude moralistic
approach has been that in both diplomacy and war it has
enabled us to make colossal blunders, and then cry out
in moral indignation against the other party for taking
advantage of our blunders. By this route, it is easy to
carry all arguments into a realm in which it is impossible
for men ever really to confront themselves with their own
mistakes.

At the opening of a war, for example, we may be acting
upon a grave miscalculation in respect of the enemy we
have decided to meet; and it must be a question whether
any belligerent in history—particularly one that had to
face a struggle for its very existence—would refuse the
opportunity to improve its advantage while it enjoyed a
temporary superiority in this way. It is true that a certain
kind of retribution may follow, since the aggressions of
the enemy are enlarged, and he may now be exposed
as even more wicked than he was before; but in the meantime the whole issue of the struggle has been monstrously
endangered and a whole continent will have suffered
unspeakable harm. Hence the cry which has so often been
repeated in Western Europe in recent years: 'We don't

want the Russians, but, if they come, of your mercy spare us from liberation.' Furthermore, once we confront ourselves with the fact that the British were planning to invade Norway before the Germans had decided on the course, it is difficult to see how the moral judgement in such an instance can avoid becoming a more dubious affair. Evidently the one power is being condemned because it succeeded in the race, while the other power—with its sins hidden in the conjuror's hat—can be excused because it only 'willed' the aggression, only looked upon the woman to lust. And this may be the case even though the power which failed in the competition was the one which had made the first move in the immoral game.

Even amongst readers of history it is probable that very few are sufficiently aware of the difficulties under which statesmen—whether of our own country or of other nations—have to carry on their work. It cannot be doubted that the world makes serious mistakes in imagining that the range of options open to a government at a given moment is vastly greater than is really the case. But statesmen do in fact come to power by claiming certain forms of skilfulness, and they operate in a world of half-truths and half-righteousnesses, in which they must assert on occasion that war itself is a smaller evil for the world than its alternatives. Some sleight-of-hand occurs if we cannot ask ourselves whether the scale of the evils in the resulting war may not be due to the imperfections of statesmen themselves. The lingering influence of ancient Teutonic sagas and romanticized war can create a mood of self-immolation in which it appears unfitting to expect prudential calculations from our governments, so that the 'war for righteousness' must be conducted blindfold. The Christian doctrine of love, however, does have one important consequence which goes to the root of this type of superstition; for it carries the implication that war as a mere holocaust—war as a useless demonstration against human sin—would be absolutely inexcusable. We could be at war as a nation every minute of our history against cruelty or oppression in some part of the world, if we did not have to calculate whether (when all aspects of the matter are considered) our intervention might not enlarge the area of atrocity or add to the total sum of human misery. Prudential considerations are required so that the cause itself should not be jeopardized unnecessarily and so that there shall be the maximum of economy in the use of so objectionable an instrument as war. Even the timing of one's entry into a conflict is a matter not to be decided by mystiques or by any Teutonic code of military honour, but by the possibilities of good or harm that will be done (or can be achieved) in the world itself. The 'war for righteousness' may produce so rigid an outlook that America is actually condemned for failing to see the absoluteness of her ethical duty from the very beginning of the War of 1914. In reality there is room for every possible gradation of judgement in respect of this matter—in respect of the moment at which a power that is outside the main controversy should make its strategic intervention in, say, a conflict between an aggressive Germany and an aggressive Russia. There can be every gradation of opinion down to the extravagance of another type of extremist, who might argue that America saved both Europe and herself by delaying her entry so long. It must never be regarded as illegitimate, therefore, to examine the actual calculations upon which a power decided and timed its intervention in any conflict. And where harm is done by an actual miscalculation, this is not to be blotted out by mere moral indignation against the enemy for taking advantage of one's mistakes. Nor is it to be blurred over by the mystique of a theory of war which pretends that what is in question is rather a species of martyrdom to be undertaken regardless of consequences. A full study of the calculations of our Foreign Office on the subject of Russia in July 1914 would be extremely relevant to any judgement concerning the origin of the First World War.

But if statesmen can make mistakes it is clear that democracies can be very wilful—very casual in respect of their responsibilities. By being comparatively disarmed in a world that was constituted like that of the inter-war period, we robbed ourselves of the power of doing good, and perhaps no statesmanship could have rectified the error or prevented colossal suffering in such circumstances. If, as we have seen, aggressiveness is always latent, and is even almost mathematically proportioned to the degree to which a state can misbehave with impunity, our relative disarmament, so long continued, was bound to be almost an invitation to misconduct. Even if our mistakes had been entirely altruistic—even if they had involved no trace of that sentimentality which becomes so powerful when combined with the interest of one's pocket, and which releases one from the austerities of a scientific attitude—those who establish openings for aggression are helping almost inevitably to create another aggressor. In other words, it is difficult to see how we can escape partial responsibility (in this and other respects) for the emergence of Hitler himself.

It is interesting to see, however, that if men's miscalculations may lure an enemy to further aggressive enterprises, the same result may also be produced by policy and design. And if in the former case we ourselves might not always have been so virtuous as we appeared, in the latter case we are not so unscrupulous as might be imagined. In the Napoleonic Wars, when the French had command of so much of the Continent while we held the seas, it seemed that neither combatant was able to reach its enemy, and a long period of deadlock occurred. We held one weapon, however; for by continuing the war we were able to prevent Napoleon's empire from consolidating itself in peace and stability—prevent it from having the chance to settle down. Compelled to continue the war, Napoleon could only march further and further in a career of continental conquest, in the hope that eventually he might ruin Great Britain indirectly. And similarly, from 1940, we produced a situation in which Hitler could not consolidate himself or restore normality, but had to be forever on the move. Twice, therefore, within one hundred and fifty years, a small island has fought continental dominion, and has compelled the aggressor to take steps that were to be his undoing. And in the process we can see how, if man first directs war, only too soon it is war which is directing man; as though a devil were presiding over the affair and securing that the original war-aims become swollen beyond all reason—each momentary success blowing them up still further until they burst as a result of their very size.

SIX

POWER AND DIPLOMACY

No question is more difficult than that of giving the right place to force and power in one's total view of history and human affairs. No paradox is more misunderstood than that of the relationship between force and an ethical order, whether in one's own country or in the field of international politics. For a long time German opinion on this subject has seemed to oscillate between two extremes: on the one side a refusal to allow force any place at all in the scheme of things; on the other side— partly by reaction—a view which seems to assume that power is the universal arbiter. In democracies there have been similar aberrations: now a belief that everything can be settled by friendly discussion around a table; and then, when a resort to force has become necessary, an inclination to imagine that mere victory in war can achieve far more—in the way of rectifying the world and improving human beings—than force is ever capable of achieving. So, in the first place we fail to realize the part played by force in the making and the maintenance of the existing order of things; and we neglect to remember a certain finality and unanswerability which power does in reality possess; since moral indignation by itself will not stop any bullets, and there is a sense in which force can be super-seded only by greater force. In the second place, however, we fail also to measure how limited are the objectives that can be attained by any mere exercise of power.

Some men would have been derisive if they had been asked to agree to the abolition of the strike weapon, and to put their entire reliance on amicable discussions between employers and employed. Yet when foreign states were at issue with one another on matters calculated to raise or depress their whole standard of living, they have imagined that mere reasonableness might be expected to prevail, and that the element of power could be ignored. In reality we know (and in certain contexts we have been prepared to confess) that in a German federal system, in which Prussia is larger, richer and more powerful than all the other members put together, the normal principles of federalism, or of 'government by discussion', become inoperative. The very international organs that we have created in the spirit of idealism at the conclusion of two world wars have conceded distinct priorities to the possessors of power. Even in U.N.O. the sweet reasonableness that comes from Peru does not in reality possess the same compelling force as that which issues from the giants of the world. And it would need blindness of an unusual perversity to deny that behind the proceedings of U.N.O. itself there is necessarily that familiar pattern which denotes power-politics. The position now occupied by the United States and Russia—and even the vast increase of their cultural influence since 1939—suggests that when men have tried to close their eyes to this problem they put civilization more completely under the presidency of power than had previously been the case.

The role of power becomes more significant if we remember that in the intercourse between states the problems which arise are not the result of mere differences of opinion on speculative matters, but are rather the consequences of diverging interests. The very aspect of international difficulty which our intellects have failed to master is just that aspect which arises from the fact that a conflict of wills—and not merely an intellectual disagreement—is involved. Ten American shopkeepers may reasonably discuss the theoretical question of Jack

K. Robinson's right to the ownership of a piece of property. The tensions become different, however, if each of the debaters is claiming the land for his own family; for now the whole discussion must transform itself into something more like a tug-of-war. New strains arise, and all relations are altered still further, if one of the contestants becomes heir to a fortune or is nominated for the Presidency of the United States. He acquires at this point what we call 'a pull in negotiation', and the introduction of power as a factor in the problem changes the character of the entire transaction. Henceforward it is a different game that is being played and there is tautness and tenseness in every move of it; for it is the game of diplomacy. One of our mistakes in recent decades has been the tendency to confuse two different things—to imagine that diplomacy was nothing more than a form of discussion, a pooling of minds, an exchange of academic arguments.

It is characteristic of diplomacy (as one of the forms of commerce between human beings) that it functions in cases where wills are in conflict and power is involved— cases where, if there were no such method of negotiation, the parties concerned would be making a direct appeal to force. And even where the struggle is a purely diplomatic one, the force of the respective states is not annulled, but is rather transmuted and transformed. That force still gives us the measure of itself, though it is turned into a kind of bargaining power, and is tamed into a mere 'pull in negotiation'—France having a stronger voice than Belgium, for example. The result is not by any means an achieved Utopia, therefore; it is simply the opening of a route by which mankind may gradually progress out of the conditions of the jungle. Men under this system make their decisions after doing a piece of mental arithmetic— after making a calculation of forces and chances—instead of enacting the full tale of violence, with the forces actually colliding and everything really consigned to the hazards of war. There have even been times when war itself has been reduced to quite small proportions, so that it seemed little more than an initial trial of strength or trial of fortune—after which the chastened combatants took their bearings afresh and resumed the method of negotiation. Something parallel to this development is apt to occur in the internal conflicts of a country, where the poor may be oppressed by an aristocracy which refuses to listen to the mere voice of reason. It seems necessary that an actual rebellion should take place—at least a single exemplary one somewhere, some time—so that the oppressed can show that they mean business, show that the situation really hurts. Once aristocracies have seen, however, that the subject classes do possess this possible weapon (and are to be treated as a 'power'), they become more ready to think of negotiation and are more amenable to persuasion. Perhaps it was from the experience of other countries that the English aristocracy, calculating consequences, learned at least to give way to the popular pressures in time. They have on occasion been able to forestall that resort to violence which would have released a flood of uncontrollable change. And this, too, is a form of diplomacy—a victory of the human intelligence in its perennial conflict with force and chance. Even though in a certain sense diplomacy is a trial of strength, it is at least an improvement on rebellion at home or carnage on the battlefield—an improvement on the blind hazards of actual war.

The achievement is all the greater in that new and more subtle aspects of power—other things besides sheer military strength—are apt to enter into the calculations when the tug-of-war is merely a diplomatic one. A state may even possess what is tantamount to 'a pull in negotiation' because, though it is weak in itself, it holds other bargaining counters, and commands other forms of influence or inducement. In the Bismarckian era, for example, Germany and Austria-Hungary were aware that they could expect little aid from Italy in time of war, but they sought the alliance of this country because they were liable to be disproportionately weakened if Italy, by taking the other side, exposed them to even a relatively slight stab in the back. Alternatively, the course of diplomacy may be complicated by the fact that subtle substitutes or oblique equivalents for force can be brought into play, such as arguments of convenience, appeals to past friendship or attempts to flatter an individual statesman. Force itself, though it may receive undue leverage when it operates by diplomatic bluff and diplomatic threat, may find its effects diluted when far-sighted statesmanship, or a reputation for reliability, is a factor in negotiation. And perhaps it is more the case in diplomacy than in war that cleverness in tactics and wisdom in strategy are able to measure themselves against the efficacy of mere power and might. If a country is in desperate circumstances, even its weaknesses may be turned into a diplomatic asset; for it may blackmail the powers into making a concession for the purpose of preventing within its borders a revolution that might be contagious. The efficacy of mere power may not be annulled or cancelled, therefore; but it can be considerably qualified or diluted in the transpositions that take place when men are playing that particular game of power which we call diplomacy. The tug-of-war is always latent, and the affair is widely different from the case of an academic discussion on the subject of the English right to be in Hong Kong. But it must always be remembered that so long as diplomacy is functioning—so long as the issue has not been consigned to the chances of war—

the human intelligence has a better purchase on the problem, a more genuine control of decisions and consequences; and reason itself still has the opportunity to work upon the governments concerned.

The fundamental part played by power in the transactions of diplomacy has often been the reason why nations have taken particular care of their armaments. It has not been the case that when they have addressed themselves to this object they have always been moved by a desire for war. We ourselves have reason to be aware that the intention may have been to prevent an aggression or a conflict; or it may merely have been to secure that due attention should be paid to what were regarded as legitimate demands. Nations which feel themselves to be weak or feel that in diplomacy they are merely on the defensive, may decide to arm more adequately because otherwise they regard themselves as failing to pull their full weight in negotiation. If you are content to remain a disarmed power in an armed world, you lack the possibility of ensuring that anybody will take any great notice of your complaints, even in time of peace. Short of some diplomatic ruse more original than the rest of the world is prepared for, it is likely that any foreign policy which you attempt in such circumstances will fail, and will come to look ridiculous afterwards; for it is impossible even to bluff an opponent when all the world knows that there is nothing behind the bluff. In that realm of international affairs in which it is impossible to satisfy everybody, but more feasible to satisfy all the states but one, diplomats sometimes seem to find that the only release from deadlock and desperation is to shift the burden of loss on to the shoulders of that party which is unable to protest. Perhaps even Germany during her relative disarmament suffered the disadvantages of this position, when certain governments, though unconvinced of the rightness of the course that was being pursued, saw more prudence in offending the powerless than in quarrelling with the strong.

It is a genuine international predicament—the result of universal cupidities and fears—which is responsible for armaments; and no system which has hitherto been tried has made good its claim to have abolished the fundamental cause or eliminated the deadlocks in human relations. It is unfortunate therefore that peoples are not induced to realize the situation and the nature of the problem—even induced genuinely to feel one another's predicament. It is true that each nation, as it adds to its armaments, understands itself to be taking precautions against that power which is the potential enemy at the moment. But we must be on guard against optical illusions; and the wildest fanatic can hardly claim now that something unique in the wickedness of Germany must be held responsible for the existence of armaments in the twentieth century. Once it is clear that another great empire can become the culprit in another decade, there is ample reason for asking whether this whole way of diagnosing the case should not itself be entirely reconsidered. It is unfortunate that peoples should be whipped into fevers and hysterias by the myth that the unexampled viciousness of a single power or a single system is the only obstruction to a general disarmament. Nobody has pierced to the hard core of the problem of international relations, or has felt the toughness of the difficulty with which we are confronted, who has failed to realize that, if Russia and all her satellites were buried under the deepest ocean, something analogous to our present predicament would quickly reproduce itself after a regrouping of the powers concerned; for it is the shadow of a common danger which gives us the illusion that all would be well if we could only blot out one of the factors in the story, and makes us dream that the rest of us would make a very nice world together if we had the entire globe to ourselves.

From many points of view it would be wrong to imagine that the concept of power in history can be eliminated by the device of turning it into some equivalent that can be measured in terms of economic resources. In the days of Hitler, when Germany said that she would have 'guns rather than butter', we were perhaps too derisory, since we have to take our reckonings in a world in which the man who possesses the guns may be able to capture the butter too. There is one error of our time which is capable of having momentous consequences; and that is the habit of comparing the economic resources of one party in an international conflict with the resources of the other combatant, on the calm assumption that the side which possesses the economic superiority is bound to win. Certainly it might win in the long run, if the long run is ever allowed to be reached; but those who risk a resort to war generally count on some device for incapacitating the enemy before he has been able to assemble more than a fraction of his resources. And the country which is inferior in economic wealth may produce a military genius or a scientific device outclassing anything possessed by the richer power. Because of this extraordinary chanciness in military conflict as such, the diplomatic tug-of-war is a more logical way of measuring relative power than any actual resort to hostilities. In this sense it steals a march not only upon the realm of sheer violence, but also upon the realm of chance. States and kingdoms often fight for strategic positions more jealously than for economic advantages, and go on fighting for power even when it means economic ruin for their people. As Acton suggested, there is no more effective cause of war than the tendency of states to go on increasing their strength and doubling their security—the sheer lust of power to expand.

These considerations are not based upon that particularly grim predicament in which we feel that the European continent happens to be standing at the present day. They represent an attempt to dig to the roots of the international problem as this was envisaged by Lord Acton in 1900, by Ranke in 1850, by Ranke's predecessors in 1800, and by students at an earlier epoch still, in 1750. They represent the situation as it was regarded in those periods which so many people seem to look back upon as better times—the situation as it existed in what we remember as the days of relative stability, when all the states of Europe were still officially Christian. It is true that in a civilized world and under a properly ordered system, the features which we have noted, and particularly the operation of power, come to be mitigated more and more. The solid framework comes to be cushioned over with the softest kind of upholstery; and human beings can achieve a relative comfort and security even under a system that has such obvious imperfections. It is true, furthermore, that the developing traditions of diplomacy, and the course of long-term reflection on the system itself, lead to the discovery of new techniques which oil the wheels of diplomatic intercourse and lead even to the emergence of what we can properly call a moral code. Since lies are so often discovered, and soon tend only to complicate the conduct of business, there comes a time when ambassadors will regard untruthfulness as outside the code—a diplomat who told lies would appear to have been a marked man in certain periods in the nineteenth century. Here, as in the financial world, the existence of confidence and credit is essential for the higher kind of business, especially the kind which envisages long-term purposes. The diplomatic profession, with its traditions and its forms of *amour-propre*, tends to make ambassadors identify their interests with the cause of peace, so that they often have a sense of failure when war breaks out, and they are jealous to see the issue taken out of their hands. Concerning the world before 1914, Sir Edward Grey once made a remark which shows how civilized the whole field of international operations can become. He said that in diplomacy it was even wrong to meet everybody with distrust—that indeed it was better to err on the side of trust than to be over-suspicious in negotiation. In these ways the art of international politics, in spite of its unpromising basis, can be brought to considerable urbanity and refinement. So much so that in the long run many people, who only see the surface of things, come to forget that there ever had been a sword behind the velvet—and imagine that the world had been naturally civilized all the time, civilized in its original constitution.

It is not the mere existence of unusual criminals that has ravaged our world; for the arrangements of society (whether national or international) ought always to presume that some of these will be lurking somewhere. The gates have been opened to evil in part because of a terrible discrepancy between human ideals and actual possibilities—terrible heresies concerning the nature of man and the structure of the historical universe. Christianity, even if it cannot persuade men to rise to the contemplation of spiritual things, embodies principles which may at least have the effect of bringing the dreamers down to earth. Because it confronts the problem of human sin, it can face our difficulties and dilemmas without evasions—without the fundamental evasiveness of those who believe that all would be well with the world if it were not for a few unspeakable criminals, always conveniently identified with the political enemy of the moment.

F

And, in particular, Christianity, throughout its history, has never evaded the question of power; though it found in martyrdom itself—that is to say, in the very extreme of impotence—a way of stealing a march on power. If Englishmen today rebel against the necessity of facing this formidable problem, it might be well for them to reflect how much more this must be the case with a resentful African, confronted by what to him must be the appalling might of the British Empire. It is useless to say: 'Here is this lion, Power; we will bring a still bigger lion to crush it.' The result could only be the predicament in which we stand today, when we see the looming shadow of the giants and monsters we ourselves have helped to conjure into existence. Short of the conversion of all men and the harnessing of human cupidity itself, what is required of us is that we should tame the lion, and steal a march on Power as we can, so that human reason encroaches on the jungle, if only inch by inch. And all this is itself involved in the progress of an advancing civilization; it needs peace; perhaps the better part of it can only be achieved when the lion is asleep. Steady conditions, historical continuity, and the healing effects of time—these are historical factors the force of which we greatly under-estimate when we try to play Providence for ourselves. It is through these that the process is encouraged by which power gives way to diplomacy, diplomacy in turn becomes more urbane, the diplomatic profession develops into an international society, and morality itself comes to have its place amongst the recognized conditions of the intercourse between states.

The makers of blue-prints are sometimes like the child who, on seeing the sunset, said: 'Do it adain, Dada'—the child who thought that it was the gardener who actually made things grow. We seek too great a sovereignty over our history; and it is wiser to imagine ourselves as rather preparing the ground where many of the most important things in life will grow of themselves. We underestimate the importance of peace and stability in this respect—the importance of peace as the necessary condition for the development of human reasonableness and for the proper balancing of the activities of men. Yet, though historians may first imagine that Colbert was the creator of a powerful economic movement, they come to realize to what an extent it was the restoration of internal stability in France which gave release to normal human energies. We begin by imagining that modern democracy springs from the French Revolution; and then we see how the steadiness of the eighteenth century and the progress of reason fostered the mentality and the ideals that lie behind the democratic movement. It is possible that the twentieth century has failed to realize the full significance of the ancient view—a view that is also connected with the Christian tradition—which sees the establishment of peace as the primary function and the supreme blessing of the body politic. Perhaps because we have come to be so far removed from the deep, elemental things in human history, we tend to think that peace is the natural, easy thing—the condition which would exist if there were no particularly evil criminals in the world, or there were no such thing as the organized state. In reality peace itself is a mighty achievement, all too precarious (as we now have reason to know), its creation and maintenance requiring not merely good intentions, but the artifice of contriving minds. We are in danger of thinking that, since peace ought to be taken for granted in any case, the function of the State may be anything in the world except the establishment and the preservation of this necessary framework for rational living. The function of the State, we think, may be to control men's labour, or to prescribe the moral end for which they shall live, or to pursue the cause of righteousness with a two-edged sword; and this enlargement of the duties of political society itself, though sometimes it is necessary, only adds to the possible causes of war. Those who conceive of peace as though it were a purely negative affair are under a serious misapprehension in any case; for genuine peace is rather like the spring, replete with forces and factors that evoke new moods and release a million spontaneities in the world; conjuring out of the bleak hillside a paradise of blossom and song.

SEVEN

AN INTERNATIONAL ORDER

A MATTER which is bound to concern us very intimately is the answer to the question: How did the régime of power politics ever come to be so chastened and qualified? If the fundamental situation is anything like the one which has been described, why in the last two or three centuries did the nations not have to be armed to the teeth all the time? In any case, how does one account for the long-continued existence of small states, which are autonomous, so that they can pursue a foreign policy of their own—not condemned to be satellites to the giant power that has the most easy access to them? It is possible, in fact, that this is the only way in which the problem of peace will ever be capable of solution—not by asking in a tone of grievance: 'Why should there be war?' but by examining the periods of international stability and asking why on earth there was not a war; not complaining that the statesmen of 1914 were so criminal, but inquiring what prevented the Austro-Russian conflict in the Balkans from breaking out thirty years earlier, as it very nearly did.

The real clue to the whole civilizing process lies in the development of an international order and the consequent release of certain 'imponderables' which seem to operate on human affairs by a species of chemistry. And it is important that we should understand this phenomenon; for it is not any international paper constitution, nor is it any particular disposition of forces in the world, but it is just these imponderable factors, which constitute the operative virtue of a supra-national system. Since it is precisely these 'imponderables' which have been destroyed in our time as the result of two world wars, we have lost the most essential aspect of an international order—the one thing that cannot be recovered by the mere drafting of a paper code. We are experiencing the usual consequences of this breakdown: foreign affairs now responding much more directly to the play of force and the shiftings of power; while measures which once were taken only during emergencies have come to be established as standing features of our world. In this situation of things, governments are under the unavoidable necessity of keeping the elastic stretched all the time. And, as Francis Bacon noted that it was harder for men to produce frost at their mere caprice than to generate heat, we today, who so easily reach high tension, must wonder why it is so difficult to bring about the converse of this. We ought, therefore, to be interested in examining the miracle by which the world ever came to enjoy the luxury of comparative low pressure—the luxury of what we have in mind when we dream of the return of 'normal times'. Christians who wish to reflect on the present-day situation may save themselves from some technical misunderstandings if they consent to examine the structure of the international order as it has existed in the past.

The historian Ranke took over from the actual practitioners of politics in preceding generations the conception of a European States-System. It was under the aegis of this particular system—and as the result of the forces which it generated—that the countries of the Continent were able to live for so long as though they were all members of the same club. The working of the system depended on the existence of a certain degree of common life amongst the nations which were partners in its benefits

—nations which had shared the inheritance of Græco-Roman culture and had grown up in Christianity. They had achieved a superiority in civilization and a supremacy in technique which secured them against any overwhelming attack from the rest of the world. By their skill or by their power, they opened up the rest of the continents of the earth and were moving towards the unification of the entire globe. Given time, and a proper realization of the required conditions, it was not inconceivable that the international order itself should be extended until it came to cover all the branches of the human race.

When Europe began to find itself in a condition of relative stability after the territorial re-distributions of the Treaty of Utrecht, there developed a clearer consciousness of the existence and importance of an international order. It came to be realized that the ultimate object of diplomatic endeavour was the preservation of this order; because, once the system collapsed, the invisible bonds which kept the planets in their orbits—kept the nations from a blind rush into anarchy—would disappear, and a general *sauve qui peut* would result. It was certainly true that, though the international order performed its function, aggression was not eliminated, and the nations still often came into conflict with one another. But it was as though the members of the international club were competing for the best armchairs or the best service at dinner—jockeying one another, shall we say, to obtain the best room in the house. And all this could take place while every single member was determined that the club itself should not be destroyed; all the parties being aware that such a catastrophe would only take away the value of the very things they were fighting about. That is to say, the governments knew that they were vitally interested in the preservation of the international system.

Even Frederick the Great was highly conscious of its significance and became a conservative defender of the system.

The subtler virtues of such a state of things were made possible by the fact that in a certain sense the international order was an aspect of the moral order itself. The effect was analogous to the difference between having a social order and experiencing the breakdown of such an order—experiencing revolution and upheaval inside a country, so that virtue loses the assistance it so often receives from the steadiness and reliability of the general environment. By operations so delicate that the superficial observer of international affairs—or the mere compiler of diplomatic history—may fail to pay any attention to them, governments and states may be restrained from the more extravagant aberrations which we associate with the condition of 'international anarchy'. Because of this there is a sense in which men, when the times are 'normal', appear to be released from some of the worst anxieties of the struggle for existence. They acquire by that very fact new preoccupations, and higher objectives; and in this moderate atmosphere a hundred 'imponderables' can work their subtle chemistry. The settled condition of the whole environment makes men run less easily to thoughts of violence against their neighbour, or policies of general overthrow.

From some date prior to the opening of the eighteenth century down to the time of Lord Acton, it is astonishing to see how much of the thought of politically-minded people was devoted to what one might call the science of the preservation of a civilized order. It was as though they knew—what the twentieth century so often forgot—that civilization is a precarious thing, a constructed thing, built on the side of a volcano, and requiring much thought even for its simple maintenance. At the time when the international ideas which we are discussing began to be significant in European history, a parallel development was taking place in respect of the methodical preservation of the social order as it exists inside single states. And here the objective was the curbing of civil conflict, so that party faction should at least stop short of the overthrow of society itself, stop short of a reversion to anarchy. In writings on international law, in the works of publicists, in the memoranda produced for foreign offices and even in parliamentary debates, other maxims were formulated, and these gave elaboration to what was really a scientific kind of diplomacy. It is not too much to say that here was a form of reflection on foreign policy the prime purpose of which was the preservation of the international order. The foreign policy of states is always more aggressively egotistical than citizens in general are permitted to realize; and those people are right who insist that diplomacy should be directed to a further end, superseding that of mere self-interest. All the same, those who in 1914-18 asserted that their zeal for righteousness would be satisfied with nothing less than the destruction of a power so wicked as Germany, were not serving any cause of love, but deifying a national hatred and walking arrogantly on the earth. There is a higher end of policy of the kind which rather curbs the passions and cupidities of states—namely, the preservation and extension of the international order itself. Even if the Germany of 1914 had entertained the schemes of aggression which the frenzy of war attributed to her, and even if it were admitted, (supposing it ever could be admitted) that a power or a body politic 'deserved' destruction, our civilization could never have been developed on the ethics of an eye for an eye and a tooth for a tooth. Those who set themselves up as the defenders of the international order are under a special obligation to curb those passions which if we examine them always so significantly comprise colossal cupidities, and to show moderation in the objectives that they put before themselves in time of war. This, not for the sake of Germany or any other culprit, but for the sake of the international order itself.

So we meet with another of those movements and processes which help to carry civilization to a higher degree of refinement—another of those developments which leave only delicate record of themselves in history. Such things are too subtle to appear in strong lines on the pages of our text-books, because their operation must be compared rather with that of the leaven which leavens the whole lump. This time it is the advance which reflective reason gains over passion, particularly over that kind of passion which is the more dangerous in that it feels itself to be so righteous. And at no point could it be more significant than where it curbs man's militancy and puts a rein on the fevers and the instincts of war—a process which we can almost say is visible to the naked eye as the international order develops at a certain period in European history.

Apart from the dislocations produced when men attempt to wipe out great slabs of power which have been part of the European system, it was long ago realized that, if there is to be an international order, all the members of it must have a real interest in its preservation —an interest which they can feel and recognize, and not merely one which somebody else tells them that they ought to possess. Otherwise it must be understood that here is a plague-spot which is bound to require the continuous exercise of force; and the total result of such a situation is not an international order at all, but the alliance of the many against the one. It is dangerous because, though all the other powers may seem united against (shall we say) Germany, the cordon comes from a temporary combination of interests and it is impossible to keep the rope taut all the time. Sooner or later a discontented member of the containing group of powers will find its interest and its opportunity in moving over to the side of the state that has been ostracized. And that is the way the landslide began in the 1930's— the way in which, in fact, the landslide will always begin.

It is time for us to shake ourselves out of the illusion that there can be an international order when one power is sent to Coventry, or one set of controversial ideas is excluded, or a great system (which is part of the effective field of forces) is hostile to the whole combination. Anybody can take out all the bulges save one in a rubber ball, or carry across the river (in the parlour game) all the missionaries save one. When we have a partial international order, its organs are only too likely to become the instruments of the victor powers; until these latter quarrel amongst themselves, so that the same institutions are turned into the instrument of one of the parties. The effective international world of today would be covered by an international order if there were a higher organ still, adjudicating between the one great section of our divided globe and the other. It is clear that we are expecting too much—and our predecessors would never have been deceived about the matter—if we imagine that communist states would be content to be out-voted on strategic issues at U.N.O. by what was known in advance to be an anti-communist majority. Even Christians, even ecclesiastical princes, even religious parties, have rejected the majority principle in such circumstances, and have preferred the resort to actual war, when vital vested interests were at stake. Nobody realizes so well as the modern revolutionary the importance of establishing stability and order within the body politic; but the revolutionary cannot achieve real consent or place reliance upon it, and therefore he knows no method save that of tyranny and force. In the international world we have fallen into the same fallacy, because we have neglected to measure the power and the importance of the 'imponderables'. The international order is destroyed because we cannot achieve genuine consent over the effective field of interrelated powers. What we have achieved with our international organs is rather a way of building up a formidable alliance in a world more divided than ever before.

Our predecessors, on the other hand, were familiar with the maxim that no power ought ever to be allowed to become so desperate—so clearly held like a cat in a corner—that, like Samson, it would pay any price for revenge, even if this meant pulling the whole house down and destroying itself along with the rest. No state ought to be allowed to be in a position in which it will decide: 'It would be better for us to re-scramble all the eggs rather than remain content with the present order of things.' In other words, when we say that an international order is based on consent, we are not using words hypocritically after the manner of propagandists and partisans. We mean that deep below all the surface-commotions and the jockeying for position, the powers do genuinely feel it to be to their advantage to belong to the system; genuinely feel that they are partners in the concern. For this reason it was realized even in the eighteenth century that an international order can never be allowed to remain static—tied to a treaty incapable of revision, for example—but is subject to violent upheaval if its machinery merely serves to freeze the *status quo*. And once upon a time it was an ordinary maxim of diplomacy that a victor should not provoke undue resentment in

the vanquished party, if there was any intention that
the settlement should be a stable one, and that the
international order, with all its 'imponderables', should
be preserved. Similarly, it was held that reformers
should move prudently, so as not to be responsible for
goading the vested interests to desperate action; or,
alternatively, that when subjects rebelled, though their
conduct might be hideous, responsibility might really
lie with the constituted authorities whose blindness
had provoked the outrages. Behind such maxims
there lies the conviction that divisions in society
should not be carried to the point where a genuine
kind of 'consent' breaks down. Also one detects the
view that we may be partly responsible for one another's
sins.

In an intellectual system which gave the primacy to
the international order, and laid such stress on its preservation, men were naturally preoccupied with the
problem of checking the aggressor—particularly the
aspirant after 'universal dominion', the single power
that might seek to dominate the whole continent. In
the eighteenth century the menace of Louis XIV was still
in men's minds and seems to have formed the basis of
reference for much of the thinking. His ascendancy, which
had led him to tyranny and aggrandisement, was the
thing which the eighteenth century particularly determined not to allow to happen again. In regard to aggression, the better minds of that age did not do what so many
English people did in 1914—did not say that only the
Germans could be so wicked, and write books of propaganda to show that the Germans had been the aggressors
throughout the ages. Reflecting (as we tried to do at an
earlier stage in this discussion) on cases of aggression that
were known in history and experience, they arrived at
something like the law behind the phenomena, and came

to the conclusion similar to that which has already been quoted from Lord Acton. And it must be said that whereas the sixteenth century is the age of Spanish hegemony, and the seventeenth is the age of French predominance, the eighteenth century prided itself in the fact that nobody could say which of the Great Powers held anything like that kind of ascendancy in its central period. To a certain degree this effect had been produced by conscious planning in the territorial redistribution established by the Treaty of Utrecht. Similarly, in the Baltic region Sweden had been supreme in the seventeenth century, holding almost all the coastline and controlling the sea; but the eighteenth century prided itself in the fact that there were now five powers in the Baltic, and no single one of them could dominate the whole region.

By the end of the eighteenth century—and possibly earlier still—the apostles of the international order had made it clear to themselves that their system was the one which preserved the existence of small states and actually gave them an important independent role. It seems to have been understood that without such a system the ordinary workings of geopolitics would eliminate the small states or reduce them to the position of satellites. It is not clear that, in the absence of an effective international order, this unfortunate process is not actually in operation at the present day. One would regard a state as a satellite if it had not the right to change its alliances, to remain neutral in time of war, or to transform its internal régime without any interference from outsiders. We should be able to tell whether Italy was a satellite or not at the present day if we knew whether any American interference would prevent her adopting communism if she desired it. In general, however, we do not sufficiently inquire how in a world of power politics the smaller countries of Europe were so long able to feel so safe, and were not forced to take desperate measures for their defence. Sometimes men have seemed to imagine that this was merely the natural and expected thing; but now we are more capable of realizing that here again there is possibly a matter for wonder and inquiry. The truth is that one can look at a cathedral, and all the parts of it may seem to be at ease and at rest—one may miss the play of invisible forces, thrust and counter-thrust, pressures and tensions and strains—so that the cathedral seems to be the buoyant expression of a spiritual mood, and even seems to be pushing upwards rather than pressing down. In just the same way, in former times people observed the small states of Europe and pictured them as nestling in their surroundings, cosy, quiet, and at rest; when in reality the apparent peace and stillness came from the operation of the international order in its entirety, and from the activity of a hundred 'imponderables' which this system generated. In part—like the peace and stillness of a cathedral—they were the product of a subtle equilibrium achieved between tremendous forces.

The eighteenth and nineteenth centuries conceived of the international order in Europe as a tremendous field of forces, which were liable to become very dangerous unless they were held in equilibrium. While the international order existed, however, it was capable on the whole of keeping itself in equilibrium; and this did not depend on whether nations happened to opt for a certain principle or not, because the principle itself tended so to speak to come into operation of its own motion. In other words, if there exists an international order, it tends to be mechanically self-adjusting and self-rectifying. As soon as the equilibrium is disturbed at any point, compensatory action automatically emerges in some other part of the system. In any case, it was judged that the rectification of any maladjustment in the system was not a difficult matter. It was possible to say: 'France has been high-handed and she possesses a margin of excess power which tends repeatedly to upset the equilibrium. We will lop off a little of this excess, if we can, so that she will have less leverage for aggression in the future.' It was not necessary to take even this course of action, however, and to destroy the whole power of France would have been a policy which contravened the code; for this would have opened the door to counter-evils, and would have implied the destruction of the international order itself.

It is easy, however, to illustrate what was likely to happen when a particular power within the international system proved aggressive. If we suppose Bavaria to be in alliance with France and assume that France happens to be the ascending power at the moment, then Bavaria naturally desires that her ally shall be successful, and she will have her eye on certain advantages which she herself will wish to draw from the victory of her partner. If we suppose, however, that France were to grow so strong as to be a general menace, and that Bavaria or other clients of hers were to feel their independence endangered, then the whole international system was fitted with ball-bearings, and Bavaria would tend to slide over to the enemies of France. This, in turn, might make the other party too strong; but in such a case some other state, feeling itself endangered, might achieve a further rectification elsewhere. No human system works to perfection, and this one did not make its adjustments absolutely instantaneously. It was not guarded against all surprises, and it could not always confront the aggressor with a sufficient combination to induce him to think the adventure not worth while.

It is not the case that the system eliminated wars therefore; and where its maxims were contravened, as in the case of the Seven Years' War, an extremely bitter conflict might result. In a sense, the Seven Years' War amply confirmed the principles involved, however; and the French, who felt that war to have been particularly significant for them—and who played an important part in the more scientific discussion of diplomacy in the latter half of the century—learned from this experience the danger of ignoring the rules. In any case, two important advantages resulted from the system, or the way of conceiving the system. First of all, that whole order not only maintained the smaller states in their autonomy, but gave them an important role in international affairs—in certain respects it gave them the key position. The small states were like ball-bearings in the system; their freedom of movement was a recognized necessity; and the multitude of them was recognized to be an advantage. If ever the world is reduced to trying to achieve the equilibrium when there are virtually only two or three parties in the arena—only two or three balls to play with, only two or three giant powers shuffling and shifting, and adjusting their relationships—then every moment of the story is bound to be particularly intense, every incident becomes a crisis, every change in the situation of one power disturbs the others, so that creaking and cumbrous machinery has to be brought into activity for minor and local occasions. And this is possibly the position at the present day, providing us with one of the reasons why nerves are kept at strain.

Secondly, in the conflicts that took place within the system, the role of war in human affairs was considerably reduced. Aggression occurred, but was not so violent or so successful as in the seventeenth century or the twentieth.

Frederick the Great was in the habit of noting in his Political Testaments the particular territories that his descendants ought to regard as desirable for the purpose of consolidating the power of Prussia. In one of these documents he cautions his successors, however; and he says that the territorial aggrandisement is not a practical policy at the time at which he is writing. The balance of Europe was working so well, he said, that even if you took the world by surprise and pounced on your object at a lucky moment, the other states would take action so quickly and both sides would soon be so evenly matched, that the war would be a very prolonged one, and if you succeeded at the finish you would gain so little that it was not worth your while to undertake the aggression. Without the slightest knowledge of what was being written in the secret Testaments of Frederick, Edmund Burke, almost at the same time, in practically the first number of the *Annual Register*, was putting forward a judgement on the international situation which follows a course remarkably parallel to this. In general, the object of war was to produce those marginal rectifications in the system which the system had been unable to achieve by its own automatic apparatus; and though of course there would be people for whom this was not at all the real purpose of the fighting, such people had to pretend that this was their object, just as powers today have to pretend that they are fighting for the current conception of what is internationally good. It was for diplomatic reasons, not for social reasons—and it was as a result of the clear consciousness of the need for preserving the international order—that in the eighteenth century there existed in theory, and in many respects in practice, the idea of limited liability wars, wars for contracted ends, wars for something short of the destruction of the enemy's power. On the other hand, the sixteenth and seventeenth centuries had seen wars of religion, wars of annihilation, wars of unlimited ends.

It may not be unrewarding to glance at the stage which was once reached by men who developed the conception of limited warfare within an international order. Their system at least came nearer than the twentieth century has done to finding some means of intellectual control over the phenomenon of war. Unless one can still believe that the middle of the twentieth century has solved the problem, it represents the most remarkable attempt to curb the evils of war—and to discipline human nature in these matters—that Europe has ever known. And there seems to be no parallel to it in the history of any of the other civilizations of the globe. It is possible to produce at least a composite picture which illustrates the lines of thought, and shows how the dovetailing of ideas does give us the shape of a coherent system; though the material must be gleaned by gathering maxims here, hints there; and now by making inferences from measures actually taken; now perhaps by reading between the lines. It would not matter if the authenticity of any item were questioned, since our purpose is only to illustrate a certain way of thinking and to show its coherency.

If it is denied that the wisdom of a former age has any validity—or can carry any suggestions—for the twentieth century, let the point be conceded for the purpose of argument, though it is not easy to concede it in respect of the type of precept which is here in question. It is useful to examine the system and the outlook, if only out of curiosity; or in order to note how far above mere partisanship is the platform from which observations are taken; or perhaps to see a kind of thinking which has grown not out of an easy utopianism, but from a methodical reflection on actual experience. In any case, it would be a complete mistake to imagine that the system merely recorded the natural practices of men at war either in an aristocratic epoch or at any period in the world's history. It represented a self-discipline and it particularly set out to counteract the palpable evils of a previous generation, when principles of an almost opposite tenour had been put into practice. In reality, its precepts are just the ones which check the wildness of our initial impulses, and call us to second thoughts, and draw our attention to long-term considerations. We might still ask, therefore, whether, if not on these lines, perhaps on some other lines, there might not be discovered a code equally calculated to regulate passion, equally calculated to soften self-righteousness, in our time. We can go so far as to say that the system which we are considering retains its validity for the society to which it applies even if only one of the parties consents to follow the rules; for it is understood that the party which desires to maintain the international order will adhere to it in case of victory, even if the other party would not have done the same.

It was often realized to what a degree wars tend to arise from deadlocks and terrible dilemmas; and how the guilt of the chief culprit at the actual moment when the war breaks out might therefore be a marginal affair. Sometimes the culprit might be particularly wilful, or might make an obviously desperate move, or might bluff and the bluff fail to achieve its purpose; but it was still necessary to examine the genuineness of the original predicament, which might contain elements of an insoluble character. It was once the case that wiser people, when talking about a war, would check a passionate verdict (particularly if it was going to have long-term effects in a treaty settlement) and would run almost as a matter of routine to the reservation: 'But here we are acting as judges in our own cause.' And this applied even when many states were parties to the judgement in question, if it happened that those states were all fighting on the same side. Almost a hundred years ago, an English minister was talking about the aggressiveness of Russia and the character of the Russian system in terms practically identical with those which are in common use at the present day. He added a word in aside (concerning the Tsar's foreign policy) to the effect that he himself would no doubt be pursuing something like the same policy if he were in the same position as the Tsar. He made it clear, however (as it was clear to all people in those days), that his understanding of the situation would not lessen his resistance to aggressive measures.

One result of our twentieth-century conception of warfare—our making the initial act of hostility the pretext for a drastic policy of general confiscation—has been the tendency throughout the whole of the war to be obsessed with the crime that originated it, so that all men's thinking is disproportionately conditioned by something that has happened in the rear. It may seem curious to us, but there is abundant material to testify to the fact that men kept greater control of the consequences of their actions when they fought their wars with their eyes upon the objective, the concrete result which they meant to produce if they gained the victory. Being possessed by no mysticism or mystique of war, they were able, furthermore, to envisage the desired end with a better grasp of the realities of the situation. They saw that, beyond its defensive objects, war can produce nothing save a redistribution of forces, and that this would be the determinant of the order of things in the after-period. It was explicitly recognized by some people that if you go to war for the possession of Alsace, or shall we say for the retention of Persian oil, it is better to announce that you are fighting for Alsace, and not fighting to secure that the power which withholds Alsace shall become more virtuous in future. It is better to say that you are fighting for Persian oil than to talk of a 'war for righteousness', when you merely mean that you believe that you have a right to the oil; for you would be conducting an altogether unjust war if for a single moment you believed anything less than this. It was realized that you can compromise about Alsace or about Persian oil, but it soon becomes a sin to compromise if you are engaged in a war for righteousness. In other words, if you possess an international order, or if it is your desire to assert the existence or the authority of such an order, you are the party which must refrain from conceiving the ends of war as though you were fighting barbarian hordes entirely outside the system. And, however bitter you may feel against the enemy of the moment, it is wiser not to be responsible for introducing a deep and permanent irreconcilability into the European order, since the enemy of today almost invariably has to be your ally against the new aggressor who is liable to turn up tomorrow. Sometimes the strain and the impulse to moral indignation between two allies is only a trifle short of the actual hostility which one feels towards an enemy. Sometimes it almost seems an accident which decides whether Germany or Russia is regarded as the prior danger at a given moment. Some prefer the former power and others the latter, but in a certain sense the giants in Europe are very much alike when they have the opportunity to misbehave, and it always seems to be necessary to use the one against the other. Indeed, human nature being what it is, there is always so much latent aggressiveness in the world that Europe could not endure unless one could use the principle of setting a thief to catch a thief. And if either Russia or Germany or anybody else wants 'total security' both now and in the future, this is to require more than Providence allows us in this dangerous universe, and is tantamount to a claim to dominate Europe oneself.

Therefore one might as well face the fact that so long as an international order exists—or so long as we might desire one to exist—wars must come short of the last degree of irreconcilability and must retain some of the characteristics of a conflict between potential allies, some trace of the fact that they are quarrels between friends. If you do not follow this policy when you have the power to do so, you are only creating a situation in which (as perhaps in 1939) you will no longer have the option, because the international order has been destroyed. Some people went so far in former days as to say that, though it was still one's duty—as much as it had ever been—not to go to war without just cause, any further insertion of the moral element into the propaganda only tended to create the evils it denounced and to add to the horrors of the conflict by giving it all the characteristics of a war of religion. Others said that it was dangerous to awaken the passions and the moral indignation of the people; for these might prevent a statesman from being able to contract out of the struggle if peace should become desirable to him for any reason. It was often realized that, if one wishes to preserve an international order, a war against an aggressor should not be carried too far in the direction of a punitive crusade. There is virtue in withholding the exercise of power even if you are in a position to act as master; and you are committing yourself to more than you realize if you try to squeeze every ounce of possible advantage from a superiority of force which is only momentary. Even territorial changes, apart from marginal ones in the case of an habitual offender, were to be deprecated on this system; and if a flood of such changes became unavoidable this meant that the war had already been carried too far. When such a thing had happened, the moment of its occurrence was the worst of all moments to choose for an attempt to stabilize frontiers and to say that no more territorial changes should ever be allowed to take place by force; for, apart from the resentment of the recent losers, a general unsettlement and fluidity of frontiers would have been produced, and a wider area of the continent than before would appear as a possible field for future aggressors. In respect of the 'collaboration' of the defeated with a victorious aggressor, Great Britain in the Napoleonic Wars—though she was brought into great distress—made it known that she would treat such complicity as involuntary, in spite of the fact that it might be carried so far as hostile action and formal war. The states involved would not ultimately be held responsible provided they helped to defeat Napoleon as soon as they were in a position to make a free choice. A further conclusion once adopted by many people in England—and not entirely uninteresting to us at the present day—was to the effect that a war against the French Revolution as such would be an unlimited war, dedicated to the policy of 'total surrender'. Therefore it was better to combat definite international offences that had been committed by the French, and so pursue a war for a contracted and limited end.

If such principles merely existed in the germ and have had to be chosen here and there for combination into a system—if sometimes they are discoverable only by implication—they represent an interesting example of the attempt to reduce the role of war in history. Behind them is the comprehension of man's universal sinfulness, and something of the sense that we are partly responsible for one another's sins. Beneath them is the endeavour which we so often think it unnecessary to make—an extraordinary striving to put oneself in the other man's place and to restrict the evils that result from our acting as the judge in our own cause. The age which developed this code was in some ways a hard one in foreign policy, and it produced many masters of *Real-politik*, or of purely technical diplomacy, who failed to keep to the rules; though in reality there was less of large-scale aggression, or 'universal dominion', or the most terrible horrors of war (save when the French Revolution restored the 'war for righteousness') than in any other period of modern history. It was an age which in spite of a growing secularism, was still near to Christianity, however—still, therefore, unconsciously influenced by some of the profounder assumptions of the religion. In a sense the whole system could be regarded as a highly elaborate projection of the idea of saving the world by an exercise of charity; for though one might be profoundly angry in war, the last irreconcilability was prevented by a merciful interpretation of offences, and a postulated forgiveness of sins. After a quarter of a century of war, and renewed war, against Revolutionary and Napoleonic France in the region of one hundred and fifty years ago—after a long struggle for existence against the most terrible usurper hitherto known, who showed no sign of stopping at any aggression, and who, after an exile in Elba, had provoked a new European war again at the very last moment—the virtues of the system led in 1815 to a treaty settlement which worked miracles in the effective reconciliation of victor and vanquished.

All this, some people will say, can have no possible relevance to the twentieth century, and we must treat it as part of the legendry of old times. Let us accept this point of view—though it passes credibility—and let us still look at the whole system, if only as though we were looking at a fossil, a mere historical curiosity. There are two things which are still worthy of note when we study this particular deposit of the European diplomatic tradition. Firstly, if we apply those older rules and the corresponding predictions to the events of our own time, those rules, those predictions of what would happen in certain eventualities, have been justified in the twentieth century to a degree beyond anything that the wildest enthusiast could have expected. We may say that the weapons are different, that democracies are a new factor, that ideologies change the terms of the problem, but the rules and predictions have shown a remarkable applicability to modern cases where colossally different weights and masses are in operation, and where completely revolutionized social systems are involved. Even in the transformed world of today, we ourselves, or civilization as a whole, lie wide open to catastrophe if we neglect certain laws which were part of the familiar outlook of our predecessors one or two centuries ago. Secondly, even if this were untrue, here is a type of thinking which deserves to be examined for its own sake; and the posture of the person who is doing the thinking is noteworthy in itself, however inappropriate the particular results may be for an age so different as ours. Not only is it the kind of thinking which chastens a man and puts a check on mere passion, but it is the kind that seeks an overall view of the problem of war, seeks an elevation from which it can embrace both the belligerent parties, and keeps in mind all the time the international order as a whole. It discovers the paradoxes, the dilemmas, the predicaments, the processes that lie behind the surface story; and it achieves certain results because it makes allowances for these. Also it provides the foothold for a science of self-criticism which is appropriate for the Christian, however difficult it may be for powers at war—criticism of that self-righteousness which seems to excuse the unleashing of the passions; and criticism of current assumptions, which is indispensable if our thought on these matters is ever to be carried to a further stage.

Clearly it is not the eighteenth century or any other period of the past which matters; and our attitude to an historical epoch or an inherited tradition ought to be flexible and imaginative. Since we cannot pretend that our own designs have saved the world from the possibility of war, there is simply a question as to whether a humbler attempt to steal a march on Power and to bridle the horses of war is a thing that should be totally excluded from our thoughts. It is useful just to know that at least a section of our diplomatic tradition reveals an attempt to examine warfare from a point of view that embraces both belligerents, envisages the international order as a whole, allows for the paradoxes in the story, and so curbs self-righteousness that maxims of a moderate and chastened kind are brought into existence. There is no question of imitating the mechanical procedures of another century. But we may wonder what would have happened to our international system if the kind of thinking which has been illustrated had grown and developed for two hundred years.

EIGHT

IDEOLOGICAL DIPLOMACY
VERSUS
AN INTERNATIONAL ORDER

THERE would not seem to be anything in the fundamental constitution of the globe which would make it inconceivable or impossible to achieve in the long run a common life and an international order on a world-wide scale—especially as all forms of communication are becoming so easy and so rapid. It will be clear, however, that the genuine bonds—like many of those which hold the British Commonwealth together—need the co-operation of time, habit, sentiment and the spirit of the club; for the imponderables are able to emerge only after long periods of normal intercourse, without undue tensions and strains. U.N.O. itself, therefore, does not stand as an international order in quite the sense that we have been using the words, or quite the sense that is required; though it is an excellent piece of machinery for helping us to knit mankind together and to build up the fabric of a united world. We may find it important not to strain the machine by insisting that the order is already here and that the system shall function rigidly on the basis of such an assumption. And we have to remember that if divisions harden, so that two halves of the globe are entirely organized against one another, the world may be more deeply sundered than was ever possible with a miscellaneous congeries of nation-states. It was even wrong for men to lose faith in the old League of Nations, for though it failed in certain spectacular matters, in which the prudent had always realized that it must be brought to its breaking-point, many of its activities had the effect of a kind of knitting process, fabricating a tradition of common action. A Canadian, speaking about the French problem in his country, once put forward the judgement that both parties to the controversy knew in the last resort exactly how far they could dare to go. They would come near to breaking-point and even flirt with danger, but a deeper wisdom would prevent them from crossing the forbidden line. Here is at once the condition and the final test of a world that stands in a similar predicament. At the last stage of the last argument everything may turn on a small pivot, therefore; everything may depend on the subtlest of the imponderables.

But the problem of developing an international order is much more difficult in fact than it would have been if we had been working with the materials that were to be found in the effective international world of 1914. It is more difficult than if we had continued the processes and extended the developments which were already there, and which required time and continuity to bring them to fruition. The obstruction to an international order is the existence of two ideological systems which regard themselves as mutually exclusive—two compounds of theory and organization which seem incapable of belonging to the same club, and which accept membership of it for the purpose of capturing its assets or for the purpose of acquiring control. Such a situation is bound to be more resistant to the establishment of an international order than any mere anarchy of nation-states could ever be. We might be tempted to say that it contravenes the primary conditions of an international system: the basic unity of outlook and the feeling of a partnership-in-the-last-resort. Those who imagine that the present situation is hopeless by definition, however, are possibly overlooking the extraordinary degree to which it has already existed in the history of modern Europe. The international ideas which we have been examining took their development partly in the reaction against this evil.

The story takes us back to a time when the right pro- pitiation of the Deity was genuinely regarded as a matter of eternal moment. The hope of Heaven and fear of Hell could govern action as powerfully as vested interests in the mundane sphere. The bond between the State and a single official religion was reckoned as a political asset of immeasurable significance. It was almost impossible for the mind to contemplate the dissolution of this mar- riage, or to see how a state could ever be divided in faith. In these circumstances, the clash between Protestant and Catholic was at once more cruelly profound and more terrifyingly disruptive than we today can easily understand. If communism is revolutionary, it hardly exceeds six- teenth-century Calvinism in its energy as a militant, missionary, expanding creed. As the headquarters of international revolution, the Geneva of Calvin presents important features which make it a remarkable anticipa- tion of modern times. The grimness of the religious con- flict of the sixteenth century reflects the fact that one system regarded its enemy as a diabolical corruption, while the other saw its enemy as a perversion, of the thing which was holiest in life. If the one was the true religion the other could be nothing more than a mask which was being used to cover unspeakable evil. In nothing were the two systems so closely agreed as on their mutual exclusiveness. In nothing was the world so ready to join with them as in the view that the two could not belong to the same club. Yet the changes in the world have been so great that today men are often inclined to see Protestantism and Catholicism almost as twins, almost as two aspects of the same thing.

Before this had happened, experiment after experiment had been made for the purpose of discovering a solution of the problem—discovering even the minimum solution which at home or in the field of foreign affairs would just provide a *modus vivendi*. If it is asked whether anything can be drawn from this chapter of human experience which might give a hint or a hope (or prove capable of transposition into the twentieth century), no doubt any attempt at an answer must depend on a subtle feeling for things, and in any case one could only leave the result angling and dangling in the mind to see whether it might find any self-ratification there. Certainly the transition was helped if, instead of pursuing a Catholic diplomacy or a Protestant policy, states worked for a limited end, giving priority to the preservation of society in days that saw terrible anarchy and bloodshed. It served a purpose even if men asserted a terrestrial morality against an alleged supernatural one, so that, while still assuming persecution to be the ideal, some of them insisted that the carnage and the battle were too terrible to be borne. In other words, granted the regrettable existence of two opposing systems, necessity drove men to put themselves outside both of these in order to take their bearings—in order to ask themselves again: 'What now is the best thing for the world?' And finally, driven to toleration, and buffeted down the road to religious liberty, they found that they could make virtue of necessity, found that freedom of conscience was not merely a compromise, but an end in itself—found therefore that they had surmounted one of the great hurdles, and broken into a new period, in the history of civilization. The process was assisted by a diplomacy of limited ends. Not a religious faction, but the interests of the international order which had been so profoundly disrupted, became the objective which was to over-ride mere egotism. It helped matters that third parties arose, equally indifferent or equally hostile to the main Protestant and Catholic bodies; also that, as time passed, the world changed in a manner in which men never remember that it is going to change. New days brought new preoccupations and new objectives so that one came into the position of not understanding why one's predecessors had been so intent on different purposes. One of the conditions of the new order of things was that Protestants and Catholics should not see in one another merely the incarnation of diabolical evil—evil so sinister that the human beings themselves deserved to be destroyed. For, in fact, the religious cleavage had produced all the phenomena of what we call Fifth-Columnism, and loyalty to a supra-national cause often implied unfaithfulness to the State. The degradation of conditions, which was the result of the whole conflict, led to those atrocities and reprisals which the men of each religious party were only too ready to attribute to the wickedness of the enemy creed itself. The world is always too little aware of the degree to which waves of extraordinary crime are due to a deterioration in conditions—due most of all to the breakdown of an order either within the State or in the world at large.

It may be fanciful or dangerous even to wonder whether any shadow of a suggestion brushes across our consciousness when we transpose this account, and read communism and anti-communism in the place of the Protestant and Catholic forms of religion. In any event, it cannot be questioned that a danger common to the sixteenth and the twentieth centuries is the fallacy of myth-making—englobing the enemy system in fog and legend, and turning it into a spectral giant, instead of analysing it into its parts. It would be particularly the duty of Christians always to remember that human beings are the ultimate units in question—human beings like ourselves, with 'limbs that will tear on a rose-bush'—who occasionally may address an indifferent half of their attention to politics. And it is fantastic to see how human beings may be trapped into what is initially a microscopic aberration; sometimes they need go no further than the error of pushing a good idea too far, without remembering the need for some counter-balance; in truth they may be at fault only in loving a good cause too much— and lo! they are committing crimes that repel us, they are soon horrifying us by their inhumanity. For this reason it is even dangerous when anti-Nazis become too like Nazis themselves, or anti-communists too like communists, in their angers and hatreds and indignations. And it is important that we should not turn communism itself into a mythical, vast, looming shape; but should examine the parts, and re-combine them, in order to discover precisely what aspect of them it is which might be calculated to make an international order impossible. There was a time when churches, in which it is now asserted that only democracy and freedom are consistent with Christianity, opposed those very objects in a vigorous and comprehensive manner. They were hostile because democracy and freedom were connected with secularism and unbelief, and, in the French Revolution, with intolerance, dictatorship, and persecution. Churchmen would have been wise not to make a mythical compound and turn it into a bogy, but to show discrimination in what they condemned.

It would be well if we could make clear to ourselves that much of what we fear in communism is not organically connected with the principle of the classless society as such. Egalitarianism itself was born out of Christian thinking, and its dissemination as a mundane ideal was the work of lapsed Christians, who took hold of a corollary of the religion, secularized it, and turned it into an end in

H

itself. It would be dangerous to allow vested interests, now on the defensive, to seduce us into such an all-round condemnation of communism as would commit us, not merely to disagreement with revolutionary changes, but to hostility against the egalitarian ideal as such, however much we may feel the danger of its indiscriminate application. Many of the evils that we hate in the Soviet system are in fact not connected with the communist ideal at all, but are rather organic to the phenomenon of revolution as such. They accompany all kinds of revolutions— democratic ones as in the case of France from 1789, Nazi and Fascist ones, and even those that call themselves Christian, such as the cases of Calvin in Geneva and General Franco in Spain. The evils include intolerances, persecutions, atrocities, high exercises of power, and even dictatorship itself; for modern dictatorship is a new kind of tyranny, born of revolution, and the communists have seen the necessary connexion between the two, though they have not convinced us that this dictatorship will ever consent to an abdication of its position. There are other evils, such as that of forced labour, which would seem to have a closer relationship to the earlier history of Russia than to the essential teaching or the ultimate ideal of communism; and it would seem to have been unfortunate that the modern implications of the Marxian system should have been worked out in eastern Europe, where civilization in general had long been in a backward state. Christians must disapprove of too great faith in mundane systems, and those who see the seamy side of human nature must be sceptical of utopias which claim to rectify the world not by altering human beings, but by remedying institutions. Some of us may feel that if society does not use the cupidities and the necessities of men in order to secure services from them, the power of the State is bound to be wielded with greater tyranny and greater possibilities of abuse in order to compel men to do their share of work. Still, it is not the egalitarian ideal as such—it is the phenomenon of revolution, the horrors attendant upon a revolutionary régime, and the resulting dictatorship—that we dread. We may even feel that, once an order has actually broken down (as in the Russia of 1917)—once the terrible smear of war has passed over society (as in much of eastern Europe in the 1940's)— the evils and horrors are going to be unavoidable in any case, so that communism may have a special function to perform, since it is clear that a liberal system cannot stand on its own feet in such emergency conditions. Even so, we do not want the horror of revolution and dictatorship in regions where there has been no break-down; and we oppose such an uprooting, not because we dislike egalitarianism, but because of all the imponderables and the subtle virtues of civilization which flourish on the continuity of history and are uprooted in these violent overthrows. Some of us would deplore such an experiment at home, because in England we still owe so much to the survival of the imponderables, the tolerances and urbanities, the many human touches and the feeling for quality. None of us could claim that the evils which we condemn would be removed if in a given country the communist régime were overthrown and the counter-revolution installed in its place. Whether we have a right to prevent other peoples from making the experiment of a revolution is a matter which raises serious issues.

In this connexion what we in England are really afraid of is the unrelenting pressure, the tireless probing and the agile aggressiveness of what we must call the international revolution. We ourselves, in our imperial capacity, are

H*

particularly vulnerable to this. At the same time, as heirs of a liberal tradition, we have embarrassed our own case in advance. England, in the nineteenth century, held that a people has the right to choose the revolutionary course; and it has often been the pride of our historians that we broke an embryo League of Nations because we objected to the use of international machinery for the stemming of the international revolution. It might be argued nowadays that we are no longer dealing with spontaneous revolution, which germinates in a natural way when a nation reaches adult status and has become politically ripe. What we now oppose is the spread of revolutionary ideas by agitators, prompted and fed by a foreign country, with Moscow exercising a presidency over universal revolt, and making itself the centre of all mischief. A new point of principle confronts us here; but it has a wide general application, and it does not exempt us from the charge of inconsistency.

When a nation like ours has developed free institutions, carefully moving in step with the advance of society and the gradual widening of political experience, it is easy for other nations to claim the same polity, because they wish to follow the example, having caught the doctrines of liberalism by a kind of contagion. If they do this at an earlier stage in their growth—before they have reached the same point in their political experience—and, more particularly, if they gain their object by revolutionary upheaval, they divide their country in a radical way, prevail by too great an exercise of power, and tend to use democratic institutions in an illiberal manner. It is not sufficiently realized that in history as in the motions of the countryside there exists a pace of maximum beauty, a pace that is itself music—the pace of the ploughman on the horizon or of the plodding barge that creeps along a canal. The progress of the liberal spirit demands this pace, for it is dependent on self-discipline and urbanity which ripen slowly and always require a moderate sun to coax them into life. The necessary tolerances come only when the atmosphere is free from excessive pressures, free from the extremes of anger, resentment, and hatred. Many troubles have fallen upon the twentieth century because in some regions democracy came too quickly, too violently, and too soon.

The so-called liberal insurrections of the nineteenth century could not have taken place without British example or French propaganda, without nests of international revolution, without all the devices of the modern agitator. But, sliding unconsciously from one moral standard to another, we in England are inconsistent as between the past and the present, and inconsistent even in respect of our own times. We who can be fervent supporters of revolution when we dislike the victim, can put the full fury of our moral indignation into reverse when we ourselves or our allies are the object of attack. And somehow, if this is the case, it can seem equally plausible to condemn the horrors and illegalities of insurrectionary politics. We then say that the trouble is due to agitators or to foreign influence, and that it is only a minority of the insurgent country which is discontented —as though all revolutions and even all improvements were not due to agitators; as though anything in the world could be achieved without them; as though the defenders of the *status quo* even in England today would have been half as liberal as they are if the level had not been forced up by the agitations and promises of the hostile party. In the nineteenth century, the revolutionary upheavals were minority movements, conducted by agitators who were in advance of their fellows; and the influences from abroad, from revolutionary France, for example, were a strategic factor in the story. Then, also, it was true that the majority of people were slow to become politically-minded; and it was recognized that, save in times of distress, they would tend to behave as an inert mass. And if the lower classes of the population in certain regions gave their support to the liberal movement it was often because they had been misled—had hoped for benefits more like those which communism promises than those which liberalism really had to offer. And some of them found themselves cheated when they saw that they had been used only to support a movement which resulted in their mill-masters acquiring the vote.

Like all holders of empire, we are more conscious of the benefits that we confer on subject peoples than of the fact that we exploit other men's lands and occupy strategic positions in them. From one point of view, therefore, we support what in other connexions we so often condemn—namely, paternal government. In this we may have much justification, and other holders of empire may have had more to say for themselves than we have sometimes allowed. We should be deeply happy if native peoples could be wiser than some of the European ones have been, and freely recognize that paternal government itself for a period might be the key to a safer and happier future. What could be more British, however, than the retort: 'Better self-government than good government'? And what answer can we make to the communist programmes of paternalism and 'guided' democracy, unless we can say: 'Liberty is the essential; it must never be sacrificed for the sake of efficient government or material welfare'?

The thing we never bargained for was the possibility that the 'war for righteousness', with all its ambiguities, its insincerities, its concealments and suppressions, would ever be turned against us. We had not thought that a voice too formidable to be ignored would ask: 'What are you Europeans doing in Asia at all?' and then would

refuse to be satisfied when we pointed to treaties con-
cluded with peoples who either had had no choice or had
suffered from an accidental inferiority in negotiation.
And when we are charged with performing a conjuring-
trick—playing the international game on rules which we
make for ourselves, and indeed altering them sometimes
as we go along—the effect is that two mountainous international systems confront one another; and in the long
run we cannot escape the ultimate challenge—the appeal
from conventions to morality itself. When the international order has broken down and the *status quo* has
been shaken on every side, all rights are more deeply
questioned and referred to first principles, so that the
customary justifications no longer meet the case.

A central tradition of English historiography and
English Whiggism once deprecated revolution, and held
that democracy should be a gradual growth, whether in
Europe or in other continents. It remembered not merely
the virtues but also the good fortune of Englishmen, and
saw that where the externals of liberty are prematurely
achieved they lead to post-democratic forms of tyranny of
a kind with which we have now become familiar. There is
such a thing as the possibility of being duped by one's
own war propaganda, however, or being carried by it to a
position of which all the consequences have not been
foreseen. Because it long suited our polemical purposes
to throw overboard the safeguards, it will not be easy for
us to maintain the plausibilities when we try to preach
the postponement of liberty in regions where our own
imperial interests are gravely concerned. In nothing did
men exult so greatly in 1919 as in that principle of self-
determination which seemed to bring the aims and purposes of the First World War to their culmination. But
leaving aside the question whether that object has really
been furthered as the total result of a generation's

endeavours; leaving aside the question whether it did not lead one into impossible situations, and whether in 1919 we did not reject its consequences even within the British Isles; leaving aside the question whether the Western Powers may not themselves be moving now to positions which will prove inconsistent with the principle we so greatly idolized—we might have done some self-questioning on this whole matter, as Queen Victoria did almost a century ago. We might have asked what it was imagined would be the fate of the British Empire if the principle were to be applied there with the genuineness and the immediacy that we were prepared to demand when it suited our purposes. It is even possible that in order to prevent Germany from having an empire we opened up a new course of critical undermining which, if carried to its logical conclusion, was bound ultimately to sap our own system; just as Catholic attempts to discredit Jansenist miracles led some men to dig further and undermine all miracle.

Let us be clear about the fact that empire is neither built nor maintained without some strokes of hard policy and without the generation of deep resentments. And if we are sometimes exasperated by officialdom even at home, can we imagine what must be the reaction of awakening minds in regions where the officialdom represents the foreigner, and the foreigner is in the country also to exploit it? Our own inconsistencies must move us to misgiving when we remember the story since 1919 of Ireland and India, Malaya and Africa, Persia and Egypt, as well as Tunisia and Algeria. And the modern form of revolution is not the cause of all the trouble, for there was Irish rebellion before the communists had established their system, and we sent the Black-and-Tans before we ever heard of Nazis. Polemical writers are quick to say that those who wish to confront squarely the problem of power are the apostles of *Real-politik*; but the situation is quite the reverse. It is merely necessary to insist on facing the plain fact that behind the apparatus of Britain's 'wars for righteousness' there has been a hard core of power politics all the time. We in this country, who can be so horrified by vested interests and strategic considerations where another nation is concerned, are too naïve to be plausible when our eyes glide unheedingly over the mountainous 'interests' we ourselves possess overseas; or we forget how easy it is to be virtuous when the cause of virtue is one that combines with our interests and provides concealment for them. The international system, as established in 1919, left Britain with its Empire, its subject peoples, and its strategic places; and there was not even as yet that freedom for the Irish for which Mr De Valera had made a moving appeal. The Empire could not be challenged without a breach of the system, nor was it admitted that the League of Nations could intervene, say, between Great Britain herself and her Indian subjects. It was to be impossible for any other power throughout the future to take the first step towards the acquiring of such an empire or such possessions for itself. To crown all, our Empire was to be maintained more cheaply than any other that has ever existed in the world's history; for if there was no complete disarmament there was to be no more stealing, and the League had been created in order to deal with any aggressor who made an attack. It was calculated that even the defence which empires had always needed against competitors was to be largely unnecessary in future; and no wonder we thought we could disarm to a great degree, for against whom could the armaments be required, save possibly the recalcitrant amongst the subject peoples? It was the most extravagant case of the freezing of the *status quo* which has ever been attempted in human history.

Compared with this, there never has been in Europe anything that could be called an attempt to freeze the *status quo*. Our great danger is that we may find ourselves today in the position of being so Metternichian that Metternich himself hardly deserves the name. And if we urge our undoubted good intentions, and the beneficent prospect we offer in an Empire which in some respects is unique, it is still important that we should not deceive ourselves about the figure we are in danger of cutting in the world. Metternich, too, thought that he could make good government a substitute for immediate self-government; and some men judged the Austrian part of Italy to have been better administered in his day than the rest of the peninsula. But Metternich knew what he was doing; while we—as the arteries harden and the crust solidifies—can take over the part he played, and go on imagining ourselves to be liberals still.

Indeed, if the principle of the 'war for righteousness', the war for the improvement of the world, is once accepted, it becomes legitimate to ask the question: Why should its operation not be aggressive? It was aggressive in the case of the French Revolution as well as in the liberal movements and some of the diplomacy of the nineteenth century. Once we have left the austerities of limited diplomacy and envisaged warfare as messianic— as a means of improving society and establishing righteousness—we have already crossed the main frontier and turned war into an instrument of policy. In any case, the culmination of the war to produce Utopia must always be—and perhaps this has already happened—the emergence of a power that will out-bid liberal democracy itself in its temptations to insurrection, its bribes to human cupidity, its standard of 'righteousness', its promises of a heaven on earth. If not now, still some day, the war for a better world, the 'war for righteousness', must feel that it need not wait for a Germany to commit an offence before it unleashes its crusading fury. And some day the 'war for righteousness' is bound to become the most sinister of all the tools of power.

It is even true to say that Russia has brought to the bitterness of its logical conclusion—and to the only logical conclusion possible—the idea of the messianic conflict, the war for the promotion of democracy. There is no escaping the fact that over a great portion of the globe at the present day—and over the illimitable stretches of Russia herself—it would be impossible to establish the Anglo-Saxon type of democracy and to work it in the authentic Anglo-Saxon way. An Anglo-American doctrine that only this genuine kind of democracy is conducive to peace, or a parallel decision that only this kind of polity can be tolerated in the world—in other words, a crusade to make our kind of government universal—would not only be based on an untruth, but would be indistinguishable from a project of Anglo-American domination. For in all the newly-awakened regions of the world the issue of such a conflict can only be between alternative types of what we might call pseudo-democracy—on the one hand, the 'guided' democracies of occupied countries (like Japan) or of British colonial areas; on the other hand, the 'guided' democracies of the type which communism establishes and to which Russia gives a similar protection. Once there is question not merely of defence, but of the spread of democracy by war, it is only this 'democracy under tutelage' which can be the issue of the conflict, whichever side may win; and the Russian form of this system possesses additional plausibilities and offers extra prizes, if only because it can present all the show of freeing subject peoples from a foreign, imperial overlord. We are doubly discomfited; for the genuine type of Anglo-Saxon democracy is just the thing that cannot be achieved by war—we cannot pretend that a counter-crusade would be favourable to the imponderable factors which are essential to the working of free institutions. Furthermore, the communists are in a position to force us at least to give the appearance of being as tyrannical as they are themselves; for if we resist them or check them they can pretend to show us up as the disciples of Hitler, and we are Fascists from the very fact that we are anti-communist. In general we have been badly caught napping; for nothing could be more frightening today than the magnitude of the appeal which communism can make to the newly-awakened peoples of Asia and Africa; and in spite of so many good intentions, our relations with the Africans, for example, are calculated to add to our embarrassment in the polemical campaign.

When all this has been said, however, it is no mere blind patriotism which must make many of us feel that backward peoples of the globe will have a kinder and smoother path to liberty, self government, responsibility, and civilization through the British system than they will ever obtain through the Russian one. But in saying this we are passing judgement once again upon the war for righteousness, the war for democracy; for who can doubt that the nations to the east of central Europe would have had an easier and gentler path to the same benefits if the war of 1914 had not so rudely torn up that part of the European map? Even if our own interests were not affected, and if we were to keep in mind only the higher values of society—only the quality of the civilization that is being produced—we should still have reason (as we have seen) for deploring not the classless society itself, and certainly not freedom, but the revolutionary procedure as such, in which there is secreted a perpetual fountain of tyrannies. Once again we are confronted with what must be one of the fundamental purposes of the

State—the upholding not of hierarchies and interests but of the kind of order which reduces the play of force in the world and gives the opportunity for the activity of reason and the imponderables. History does not seem to me to suggest that we need despair, even in the face of the international revolution, provided we are concerned to defend the higher values of civilization rather than to buttress vested interests. The story of sixteenth-century Calvinism shows that a 'contained' international revolution may settle down in time to routine and a kind of conservatism, as human beings move into a world of new preoccupations. The story of the nineteenth-century international revolution demonstrates that men like Bismarck and Cavour, and even the European monarchs themselves, were able to strengthen their systems and 'contain' the enemy by stealing the best weapons of the revolution itself—facing the fact that mere conservatism and resistance are useless.

As we cannot expect on the top of everything else that we should hold something like an empire without resistances and bitter agitations, we might say that we could not complain at the present day if what we were faced with were only the legitimate spread of communist ideas and liberty movements. The real anxiety of our position is the product of a different group of factors—namely, those which are the effect of the unparalleled predominance which has recently been acquired by Russia herself. If we fear for our civilization today, that is because every new victory of the revolution adds to the power of Moscow and increases its ascendancy in Europe and in Asia; while the new momentum of the attack itself springs from the strength and prestige of Russia since 1945 —springs from the new weight that she can now throw into the balance. These factors were not effective in the 1930's, and a communist revolution in that period would clearly have failed to arouse the peculiar alarm which it would give us at the present time. In that decade the liberals spoke so kindly sometimes concerning the faith of the communists that it has been an embarrassment to see their words thrown back at them in the Marxist propaganda of recent years. It is the power of Russia and the new disposition of forces in the world since the Second World War that has made the difference both in the movement itself and in the attitude we adopt towards the spread of communism. And here is an example of the way in which the net result of a war (after defensive purposes have been served) is precisely its effect on the distribution of power. We can hardly claim that communism in Moscow has suddenly changed its character, though sometimes we might wonder whether tyrannies and atrocities do not begin in a country from the moment when that country becomes a potential enemy and a mysterious hand turns on the atrocity tap. And if we are correct in saying that it is the communist ideal as such which is the seat of the evil—the ultimate source of aggression—then Hitler (with Russia so much more nearly on the top of him) must have been more right about this in the 1930's, and we more wrong, than we have been prepared to admit. It is important for us to make clear to ourselves that it is Russia—it is this great slab of power, now possessing the ability to attract more power to itself—which is the real seat of our post-war difficulties. And not only would a Russia so dominant on the continental land-mass have shown all the same abuses of power in Tsarist times, but it was realized beforehand that she would do so, as soon as she found that she could take action with relative impunity. The Soviet system may have added to her efficiency since Tsarist days, and the Marxian theories may have proved more advantageous than the ideologies and excuses then at hand. But, then, as now, power is short of no excuses when it can act with impunity, and we are brought back to the point where we began—to Acton's point about the tendency of unchecked power to expand indefinitely.

We may condemn atrocities, we may condemn revolution, but it is not permitted to us to judge the actual ends of a revolution from the atrocities alone. If we do this, we are in danger of repeating the mistake of those people who in former times condemned not merely the French Revolution, but democracy itself, because of the Reign of Terror. The procedure has a further disadvantage in that it puts us in the danger of deceiving ourselves in respect of certain things in which even communism may stand as a reproach to us. It is not sufficient to see intolerance, persecution, and atrocity and turn away with loathing; for that is what men do with the Christian Church, which in these particular respects has a sorry history to live down. We may take a superficial view of contemporary Russia and say, 'These men are devils', and there may be some truth in the allegation; but if we think that we have thereby disposed of communism, what shall we say to the secularists who rightly see sixteenth- and seventeenth-century Protestants and Catholics in the same light? It is not clear that since the Renaissance there are excuses for religious atrocities—by reference to the state of civilization or to politico-ecclesiastical necessities—which would not apply perhaps even *a fortiori* to the modern communists. The communist ideology is a formidable one; and it is a question whether we of the Western world generally are opposing it with a counter-system that has been thought out with any thoroughness. And communism is a Western product—it has become the means for a Westernization of the world more rapid than the British Empire ever thought possible or pretended to achieve. Even its evils represent that kind of 'modern barbarism' which continues the lines of development we have only too often had to deplore on the European continent as a whole. And in a sense we are all nearer to communism than we imagine—for in regard to social arrangements we have been moving in some respects in the same direction, however unwilling we may be to move quite so far. The charges which Christianity has to make against communism—the atheism, the materialism, the intolerance, and that conception of human life on the earth which harnesses and enslaves man to the exploitation of the resources of nature—are a momentous matter, and would increase (if anything were needed to increase) our resolve to defend our own civilization. But these things are not to be reduced—they are more likely to be increased—by a 'war for righteousness' against them; and in any event Christianity has a prior case against Western Europe itself, as the source of these very errors. If there were a war which in any sense could be interpreted as an attempt to confirm the exploitation of Asia and Africa by the white man, it is of the greatest moment that such a war should not be allowed to disguise itself as a Christian crusade against atheism. And if we are to judge by the two world wars of the twentieth century, a crusade against communism would be the surest way of establishing that very system over vast new areas of the world.

It is not, then, a 'war for righteousness' against communism—not the erection of a great Christian counter-system or the installation of a militant democratic crusade—that the present situation can ever call for; and we must feel half-afraid lest our American associates should be unimaginative in their self-righteousness. We could afford to tell the Russians that we would not have allowed them to steal so many marches on us as they have tried to do, even if both we and they had been Christian nations in the traditional meaning of the term. We are doing what the Russians want us to do when we make our diplomacy ideological; for where the appeal is to mass opinion the defenders of the *status quo* are under a handicap, since they depend on the ability to carry to its final stages a comparatively subtle piece of argument. The technique of modern totalitarian warfare is to exploit superficialities and to make play with the obvious catchwords; and one may be right on a profound and far-reaching analysis of the situation, but woefully vulnerable because on a first hasty glance one appears to be in the wrong. If we stand for anything, we stand for the right of states or individuals to adopt Catholicism or Protestantism as their creed, and to establish the classless society or to prefer even paternal government. We stand for the right to resist intrigue and insurrection when they threaten us; and the right to defend our own order even against another order that claims to be better than ours. And this means that we abandon the whole programme of the 'war for righteousness', and reject both revolution (in the sense of insurrectionary politics) and war itself as instruments for achieving good in the world. It means that we will not only refuse to begin a war until we are compelled to do so, but we will only continue it so long as the enemy insists upon it, or so long as is necessary for defending an order to which we are generally attached. It will not be our object to produce the overthrow of the order already existing in other countries, or to pull up any more plants or systems by the roots; especially as we know that the annihilation of communism is a matter of the greatest unlikelihood, whatever may happen to Russia. If ideological warfare and ideological diplomacy were right, we should have to go one step further and agree with the Marxists in the view that civil war is more important than foreign war—international conflicts must then be turned into intestine struggles too, and all the bitterness must be multiplied. In reality, supposing war were to prove unavoidable, many people would fight in defence of their country and their civilization with less misgiving if the war were a limited one, not mounted as a religious campaign against wrong, and viciously supercharged.

An international order which shall include communism and the Anglo-Saxon democracies is no impossibility if the former is 'contained' and the nations so settle into the terms of the new situation that the revolutionary stage in various countries is surpassed. For it is not communism as such, but the revolutionary stage of present-day communism which is the danger; and Protestantism and Catholicism tended to behave in the same way when they were in the same position, for they too could easily think themselves into the state of mind in which it seemed illogical for them to admit that any other system should have the right to exist. Nothing, therefore, could so hinder the establishment of an international order as the settled policy of seeing in communism itself— and particularly in the classless society—the arch-enemy and the seat of all evil, or the headquarters of the last remaining wickedness in the world. The Russians may treat us in that manner, but it is we who wish for an international order—wish for a system which shall have room also for them. To say that we would not live with communism even if it was willing to allow us to do so would be a negation of the international order—and this is what ideological diplomacy really means. Moreover, here is one of the occasions when, if a single party to the quarrel can discipline itself, the effect may make all the difference in the world.

Forces which we may describe as almost daemonic in character can certainly seize upon communism, as they seized upon democracy itself in the days of the Reign of Terror. And we see these forces at work in the Nazi movement, in Palestinian atrocities, in the conflicts of religion, and in totalitarian war. We may even say that these forces, and the resulting evils, are closely associated with those regions of breakdown and upheaval which have produced the phenomenon of modern barbarism. Christian history itself has not been free from the same burden of horror when churchmen have so held their religion as to provide a foothold for the daemonic powers. But Christian charity is the grand and mighty exorcism, and it should induce us to examine the superimposed forces or study the conditioning circumstances. For our highest object is not to fight or to kill (except as they themselves insist upon it), but rather to rescue the men who sometimes in a wholesale manner seem to have become the victims of diabolical agencies.

3/10/54